THOUGHTS
FOR
THERAPISTS

PUBLISHER'S NOTE

This publication is designed to provide accurate and authoritative information in regard to the subject matter covered. It is sold with the understanding that the publisher is not engaged in rendering psychological, medical, or other professional service.

Books in The Practical Therapist Series® *present authoritative answers to the question, "What-do-I-do-now-and-how-do-I-do-it?" in the practice of psychotherapy, bringing the wisdom and experience of expert mentors to the practicing therapist. A book, however, is no substitute for thorough professional training and adherence to ethical and legal standards. At minimum:*

- *The practitioner must be qualified to practice psychotherapy.*
- *Clients participate in psychotherapy only with informed consent.*
- *The practitioner must not "guarantee" a specific outcome.*
      — Robert E. Alberti, Ph.D., Editor

Other Titles in The Practical Therapist Series®

Anger Management
Anger Management Video Program
Creative Therapy with Children and Adolescents
Defusing the High-Conflict Divorce
Divorce Doesn't Have to Be That Way
How to Fail as a Therapist
Integrative Brief Therapy
Meditative Therapy
Rational Emotive Behavior Therapy (Second Edition)
The Soul of Counseling

The Practical Therapist Series®

THOUGHTS
FOR
THERAPISTS

REFLECTIONS ON THE ART
OF HEALING

BERNARD SCHWARTZ, PH.D.
JOHN V. FLOWERS, PH.D.

FOREWORD BY ARNOLD A. LAZARUS, PH.D., ABPP

Impact Publishers®
ATASCADERO, CALIFORNIA

ATTENTION ORGANIZATIONS AND CORPORATIONS:
This book is available at quantity discounts on bulk purchases for educational, business, or sales promotional use. For further information, please contact Impact Publishers, P.O. Box 6016, Atascadero, California 93423-6016. Phone: 805-466-5917, e-mail: info@impactpublishers.com

Library of Congress Cataloging-in-Publication Data

Schwartz, Bernard, 1943-
  Thoughts for therapists : reflections on the art of healing / Bernard Schwartz and John V. Flowers.
     p. ; cm. — (The practical therapist series)
  Includes bibliographical references and index.
  ISBN-13: 978-1-886230-74-3 (alk. paper)
  1. Psychotherapy. 2. Healing. I. Flowers, John V., 1938- II. Title. III. Series.
  [DNLM: 1. Psychotherapy—methods. 2. Aphorisms and Proverbs. 3. Professional-Patient Relations. WZ 309 S399t 2008]
  RC480.S333 2008
  616.89'14—dc22

                                                    2007027576

Impact Publishers and colophon are registered trademarks of Impact Publishers, Inc.

Cover design by Gayle Downs, Gayle Force Design, Atascadero, California.
Composition by UB Communications, Parsippany, New Jersey.
Printed in the United States of America on acid-free, recycled paper.
Published by **Impact 🖋 Publishers®**
POST OFFICE BOX 6016
ATASCADERO, CALIFORNIA 93423-6016
www.impactpublishers.com

Dedication

To those profound thinkers across the oceans of time who have captured the many faces and features of the therapeutic endeavor.

— Bernard Schwartz
— John V. Flowers

Contents

❖ *Section VIII*

Evolving Perspectives on Therapy   *101*

Foreword

One of the biggest problems with clinical psychology and psychotherapy is that practitioners often use methods that "feel" right, or make intuitive sense, despite the absence of empirical support.

As a result, the science of psychology and methods of clinical practice frequently fail to connect. The practice of therapy is as much an art as a science; there is room for creativity and innovation. However, when clinicians rely almost exclusively on artistry or intuition and ignore the scientific side of the equation, the best interests of consumers are rarely served.

Fortunately, some new developments are pushing mental health science and practice closer together. More and more studies point to empirically validated treatments for specific disorders and, even with its drawbacks, the behemoth managed health care system is promoting evidence-based treatments, often declining to reimburse practitioners who use unproven methods.

So where does clinical intuition fit into this picture? Perhaps the best piece of advice I received early in my career was from a supervisor during one of my internship rotations at a day hospital in London. "Be yourself," he said, "but examine your feelings." In other words, don't be a slave to some strict theory, don't just go by the book, trust your intuition but not without questioning it, and remember to keep your brain in gear. Sage counsel, and I offer it as valid today as it was nearly five decades past.

But are we born with "intuition" worth trusting? I think not. Rather it is honed by training, by life experience, by common sense, and by reading and listening to sage counsel from wise elders.

And that's where *Thoughts for Therapists* comes in. Bernie Schwartz and John Flowers have put together an amazing collection of "sage counsel from wise elders." Their thoughtful, thorough, well-organized volume offers a rich collection of the best thoughts of the best thinkers in the field of psychotherapy. Moreover, they have incorporated the perspectives of great minds from related fields into the project — philosophers, neurobiologists, poets, coaches, writers, humorists.

At those critical moments when we as clinicians need reassurance, encouragement, and inspiration, here is a resource we can turn to with confidence, knowing we'll probably find words that can guide us as we develop professionally, struggle with difficult cases, adapt to changing times.

Yet this book offers not only resources for specific clinical issues, but a source of therapist self-care one can consult again and again over the lifelong professional path from novice to expert. You'll discover vivid word pictures of the essence of what it means to practice the art and science of the profession of psychotherapy.

Needless to say, I don't agree with all of the intellectual viewpoints presented in these pages. While my own multimodal therapeutic perspective incorporates much from the work of others, I have always insisted there be a solid foundation on that "scientific side of the equation." Thus, I'm much more often in agreement with Beck, Ellis, and Bandura than with Freud, Jung, or Yalom. Yet that may be one of the greatest strengths of *Thoughts for Therapists*. This slim volume brings together thinkers on all sides of the issues psychotherapists face. You are presented here with stimulating arguments, refreshing ideas, unresolved controversies, and other food for your own thoughts, insights, and judgments.

Fill your plate, again and again!

> — Arnold A. Lazarus, Ph.D., ABPP
> Distinguished Professor Emeritus of Psychology,
> Rutgers University and
> Executive Director of The Lazarus Institute,
> Skillman, New Jersey

Introduction

Words and magic were in the beginning one and the same thing and even today words contain much of their magical power — by words one can give to another the greatest happiness or bring about utter despair. Words bring forth emotion and are universally the means by which we influence our fellow creatures.

— Sigmund Freud

When the Greek playwright Aeschylus (525–456 B.C.E.) declared, "Words are healers of the ill-tempered," he captured the essence of doing therapy. Words are what we use to reassure, to encourage, to confront, and to inspire our clients. But what about the times when we as clinicians need reassurance, encouragement, and inspiration? Where are the words that can guide us as we develop professionally, struggle with difficult cases, adapt to changing times? Certainly, colleagues, mentors, and professional seminars are indispensable as supports. However, over the years in our work supervising graduate interns, we often discussed how useful it would be for our students to have a reference work available that contains the best thoughts of the best thinkers in the field of psychotherapy — one that addresses the breadth and depth of what it means to be a therapist. And thus an idea was born.

But where to start? Thank goodness for academic databases and the Internet. These technologies provided us with access to hundreds of books, old and new, as well as thousands of journal articles. The search became a treasure hunt for those little kernels of wisdom that might illuminate some aspect of doing therapy — and we were not disappointed in our efforts. What we found was that many master therapists and researchers were also master communicators, able to simplify the complex, make concrete the abstract, use language that was poetic and profound.

As our search expanded, we also incorporated the perspectives of great thinkers from related fields into the project. Thus, *Thoughts for Therapists* also includes the words of philosophers, neurobiologists, poets, coaches, and humorists.

❖ *How to Use This Book*

Like other books of quotations, *Thoughts for Therapists* can be read in a random manner. Open a page anywhere and you can reflect on a useful "thought for the day" before plunging into your clinical practice. However, our goal in writing the book was a little loftier than providing a mere collection of profundities. We wanted to address a number of therapeutic themes that are at the core of doing clinical work — themes that have been written about extensively — and that is the problem: Who has time for reading extensively about the ever-increasing array of therapeutic concerns?

Thus, we designed the book to be useful as a brief reference work for when specific clinical issues arise. If, for example, you have been experiencing frustration with a client's lack of progress or, heaven forbid, premature termination, there are passages that illuminate the various challenges clinicians face. If the therapeutic relationship with a particular client is unsatisfying, there are sections that explore the actions and characteristics of effective clinicians. Other sections explore the need for therapist self-care and the lifelong professional journey from novice to expert.

Finally, we discuss several of the emerging trends within our field: the rise of "positive psychology" as an alternative to pathology-based orientations; the integration of Eastern psychology (the Far East, not New York!) into the mainstream of clinical work; and the constructivist view, which incorporates developmental psychology's concept that the individual can assimilate and accommodate changing experiences.

As action-oriented clinicians, we felt that it was not sufficient to simply collect and discuss a variety of reflections by renowned therapists and other writers. We believe that cognitions are most useful when they are guideposts to behavior. Thus, following each section of quotations we describe a "Case in Point" drawn from our own clinical work, which hopefully connects theory and practice, and a section titled "Putting It into Practice," which provides concrete suggestions for enhancing one's clinical practice.

We hope this book becomes a welcome professional companion, one to which you frequently refer for insight and guidance on your journey as a healer.

On the Therapist's Challenges

They hope we will help them restore their morale — that is, both their belief that the world and life can be a good place for them [again] and their faith in the goodness of humanity or themselves.

— Ronald Miller (2005)

A master therapist makes it look easy. Mix together a little active listening, some goal setting, encouragement, a clever assignment here and there, and voilà! the client's problem is resolved. In this section on the challenges therapists face, we see that there is much more to therapeutic effectiveness than meets the eye. Perhaps that is why there is such a high dropout rate from therapy — 20 to 57 percent of clients do not return after their first session (Cross & Warren, 2004). This startling fact is understandable given that the factors leading to successful outcomes in therapy are many and the obstacles to achieving those outcomes are even greater.

Fortunately, many decades of research and reflection have provided us with a number of insights into the art of healing those who come to us bearing wounds of hurt, fear, and failure. We now better understand the challenges we face, the actions that promote healing, and the characteristics we must embody as therapists. And most of all, we now know that therapy cannot be impersonal or formulistic, that it requires a genuine human connection if it is to succeed.

❖ *The Complexity of Clinical Work*

To understand individual patterns within the multiple patterns of the human condition — the most complicated of all species — is to take on a task of immense proportions. This putting one's arms around the human condition and its many expressions is like saying, "I want to get to know the pattern of each snowflake or all cloud combinations or the songs of birds from everywhere."

— Thomas Skovholt and Len Jennings (2005)

Building the human brain is vastly complex, rebuilding it is a difficult and fascinating challenge.

— Louis Cozolino (2003)

Canst thou not minister to a mind diseas'd
Pluck from the memory a rooted sorrow?
Raze out the written troubles of the brain?
And with some sweet oblivious antidote,
Cleanse the stuff'd bosom of that perilous stuff which weighs upon
*   the heart?*

— Shakespeare (Macbeth [5, 3, 50–55])

Wouldn't it be nice if we could simply pluck out the pain of our clients as Shakespeare would have it? Alas, although doing therapy may not be brain surgery, it is perhaps the closest thing to it. Unlike neurosurgeons, however, we do not have computerized tomography and positron emission tomography scans to help us find our way during the clinical process. Certainly we have diagnostic and assessment tools, protocols, and clinical experience to help guide us, but the complexity and variety of human function and dysfunction present an infinite array of obstacles and challenges. The good news of doing therapy is that you never know who will show up next in your waiting room. The bad news of doing therapy is... you never know who will show up next in your waiting room: perhaps a run-of-the-mill case of performance anxiety; maybe an abused woman, alone in a foreign country, desperate to escape her abusive husband, yet so culturally bound she dare not leave; maybe a teenager who is skipping school and smoking pot; or maybe a ten-year-old adopted refugee from Africa...

❖ A Case in Point

P.J. had been living on the street in Kenya for several years. His daily routine included petty crime, sniffing glue, and warding off thugs. A caring couple in the United States concerned about the plight of such children adopted him into their suburban home expecting...well, not knowing *what* to expect. They brought P.J. to therapy after he had repeated episodes of night terrors.

Such cases remind us of the complexity of human existence in the "global village" and the awesome task we have undertaken as therapists. And so sometimes with confidence, sometimes with trepidation, we join our clients' journeys, working to provide the missing pieces — the hope, the support — that can make them whole again.

❖ Putting It into Practice

Be prepared for cases that appear simple on the surface but contain greater complexity than anticipated. For example, a "simple" case of social phobia can be complicated by the fact that often the therapeutic situation itself is a painful social encounter for the client.

> *The person with social phobia may thus censor information, engage in subtle avoidance in the therapy situation, or act in a manner that is distracting to the therapist.*
>
> — Nicholas Tarrier et al. (2000)

Recognize that standardized treatment manuals for emotional disorders may be good starting points for finding treatment methods, but these methods often require significant modification when applied to specific individuals.

> *Therefore if manuals have not made a significant impact on the therapist's performance in controlled research settings (for which they were designed), it is highly unlikely they will have a noticeable impact on real world practitioners.*
>
> — Jeffrey Binder (2004)

"Know what you don't know." No one therapist can be expected to be a master clinician in all therapeutic domains. The era of the general practitioner in psychology has passed, and more and more clinicians are developing subspecialties that require expertise and ongoing training. Trauma work, custody evaluations, eating disorders, and sexual abuse are but a few such specialty areas. Therefore, we must be ready, willing, and able to consult and refer when cases stretch beyond our knowledge base.

> *We as therapists must consider our own limitations, who we are as people, what we represent, and the prejudices and biases we bring to the [clinical] relationship.*
>
> — Malcolm Cross (2001)

Remember your clients are not reducible to a mere diagnostic label. A diagnosis does not define the person or tell you all you need to know to develop effective interventions. The complexity of human beings leads us to consider the totality of a person, including the client's strengths, goals, support system, personal beliefs about the self and the world, and level of commitment to change.

> *Any limiting categorization is not only erroneous, but offensive, and stands in opposition to the basic human foundations of the therapeutic relationship. In my opinion, the less we think (during the therapeutic process) in terms of diagnostic labels, the better.*
>
> — Irvin Yalom (2003)

❖ *Client Resistance*

> *We resist change even more passionately than we seek it. We are sometimes desperate in our quests for different ways of being, yet we gravitate toward old and familiar patterns.*
>
> — Michael Mahoney (2005)

> *The major source of resistance is . . . the feeling of worthlessness which clients often associate with abandoning their established methods for deriving feelings of belonging and significance. Clients may only abandon maladaptive strategies when they have acquired new, more adaptive, strategies . . . when they feel confident that these tactics will work.*
>
> — David Perry et al. (1986)

I learned long ago never to wrestle with a pig. You get dirty and besides, the pig likes it.

— George Bernard Shaw (1856–1950)

In ancient psychological times (about a hundred years ago), when clients did not want to do what the therapist thought they should, there was but a single explanation available — it was a simple matter of transference; that is, the client's unwillingness to follow the therapist's advice or interpretations was seen as an unconscious response to early authority figures. Today, there are a number of perspectives on this ubiquitous phenomenon. First of all, resistance may be related to a failure to form a positive therapist-client bond. This can occur when therapists do not communicate sufficient warmth, concern, or competence. Resistance can also occur when inappropriate therapeutic assignments are given: perhaps the task is too large a step; perhaps we have not clearly stated the rationale; perhaps the client doesn't have the requisite skills or knowledge to complete the assignment.

How often do we suggest an out-of-session activity such as journaling only to find out the following week that our conception of journaling bears little resemblance to the client's? Yes, sometimes the traditional notion of client resistance may be operative; however, as a rule of thumb it is probably best to follow Occam's razor, which advises that we seek the simplest, most direct explanation for events — including a client's lack of ascent to our insights and recommendations. In other words, resistance may indicate that we are actually off the mark in our interpretations or that we are recommending "too much, too soon."

❖ A Case in Point

Josie returned to therapy once again having failed to complete her "out-of-session" activity. Dr. Williams took great pains to ensure that she would join an online dating group and send an email to a prospective match. Given that Josie was rather shy, Dr. Williams worked hard to have her relax and visualize herself sending off an email until she felt comfortable doing so. Frustrated with the client's lack of follow-through, the therapist was convinced that this was a clear case of resistance. "Do you see how this fits your pattern of resisting authority?" Dr. Williams offered. "Actually, doctor," Josie responded, "after all your hard work having me practice until I felt comfortable, I just didn't have the heart to tell you — I have no access to a computer, and if I did, I wouldn't know what to do with it."

❖ Putting It into Practice

Consider that there may be a variety of reasons for client "resistance." Psychodynamically trained therapists tend to see resistance as being related to transference. Cognitive therapists often see it as an example of irrational or distorted thinking. However just as often, resistance, client criticism, or missed sessions may indicate that the therapist is not demonstrating sufficient empathy or is moving too fast with "assignments" or making invalid interpretations.

I think a lot of what is seen as resistance is really a reflection of misunderstanding and inflexibility on the part of the therapist . . . and often reflects legitimate concerns on the part of the client. We should take their resistance seriously and validate it.

— William Hudson O'Hanlon and Bill O'Hanlon (2003)

Take account of your client's tendency to accept or resist therapeutic guidance. Just as some athletes are more "coachable" than others, some clients are more comfortable accepting advice or direction, while others who are more oppositional enjoy a battle of wits with those in authority positions.

Having a low tolerance for being controlled by others is a special problem for patients in psychotherapy, since psychotherapy is inherently an experience which threatens one's sense of self-control.

— James Dillard and Michael Pfau (2002)

Use techniques that de-emphasize the therapist's power and efforts to change clients when working with those who are highly resistant.

The therapist is well advised to counterbalance the patient's level of resistance with procedures that de-emphasize the therapist's power and efforts to change the client. The use of nondirective, supportive,

self-management and paradoxical interventions are examples of
procedures that serve this function.

— James Butcher (2002)

❖ *Clarity of Communication*

Between what I think,
What I want to say,
What I believe I'm saying,
What I say,
What you want to hear,
What you hear,
What you believe you understand,
What you want to understand,
And what you understand,
There are at least nine possibilities for misunderstanding.

— François Garagnon (1999)

A screenwriter, speaking to movie producer Sam Goldwyn:
  Mr. Goldwyn, I am telling you a sensational story. I am only
  asking you for an opinion, and you fell asleep.

Sam Goldwyn:
  Isn't sleeping an opinion?

— Joey Green (2001)

I'm just a soul whose intentions are good.
Oh, Lord, please don't let me be misunderstood.

— The Animals (1969)

One of our most daunting tasks as clinicians is to make sure
that the messages we send to clients are the messages they receive.
Too often we use vocabulary that is overly academic, or we get so
carried away with our own verbosity that we lose the client's
attention. Sometimes we use "pathologizing" words such as
"victim" instead of terms like "survivor" that imply hope and
capability. Studies show that over 70 percent of mistakes made
in the workplace are the result of poor communication (Holm,
2006). How many therapeutic mistakes are made from poor
communication we can only speculate. But we must certainly

choose our words and nonverbal signals carefully; for, like political candidates, what we say will be forever remembered, quoted, and reflected on. Such was the case when Senator John Kerry attempted a joke that he meant to ridicule President Bush but stated it in such a way that it appeared instead to denigrate the troops fighting in Iraq (Kerry, 2006). Clinicians can also pay a heavy price when their words are misconstrued.

❖ A Case in Point

Roger, a depressed client, remarked as he headed toward the door following his first session, "My wife thinks I may need antidepressant medication. What do you think?" At first the therapist responded with the standard "We'll have to talk about that next time." However, reluctant to leave well enough alone, he then added, "I am a psychologist and can't prescribe antidepressants, but I work with a couple of psychiatrists who are good with medication, and if it seems appropriate we'll put you on antidepressants for a while." It seemed like a harmless enough statement. However, at the next session Roger was clearly less open, less enthusiastic, and less connected than previously. When the subject of medication came up again, Roger clearly indicated what was wrong.

"When you said you and the psychiatrists were going to 'PUT' me on medications it made me feel like I would have no control or say in the matter." One small word — and one giant step backward in building the therapist-client relationship.

❖ Putting It into Practice

Leave time at the end of sessions for a "wrap-up" question or two in which you ask the client what was useful in the session and what was confusing. Patricia Cross's research with college students found that using "summary questions" at the end of lectures greatly enhanced the retention of complex lecture material; this approach can be useful in therapy as well.

Having students process and restate what has been discussed transforms learning from the passive to an active state which in turn increases the likelihood of deeper learning.

— Patricia Cross and Mimi Steadman (1996)

Avoid closed-ended questions when assessing whether a client understands important concepts.

When asking for feedback, therapists overutilize such questions as: "Does that make sense?" To answer in the negative clients are forced to admit a lack of cognitive capability which can be embarrassing. Better to ask open-ended questions such as: "What in our discussion might be useful for you?"

— Paul Wachtel (1993)

If you and the client agreed on out-of-session activities, review the specifics to ensure you are on the same page.

Oftentimes we assume that our clients have a clear understanding of a homework assignment, only to find out at the next session that the instructions were completely misconstrued, sometimes with negative consequences.

— Nikolaos Kazantzis and Luciano L'Abate (2007)

❖ *Maintaining Boundaries*

Learning an optimal level of attachment — in which the practitioner experiences the world of the other, but is not overwhelmed — is an essential professional skill and a complex one. Learning how to regulate and modulate the level of emotional attachment in the curative relational process takes time. It is a paradoxical skill — learning how to be emotionally involved yet emotionally distant, united but separate.

— Thomas Skovholt (2005)

It is usually inadvisable to disregard strict boundary limits in the presence of severe psychopathology. . . . But those practitioners (and, regrettably, they are not few or far between) who impose rigid limits across the board will fail to help people who might otherwise have benefited from their ministrations.

— Arnold Lazarus (1997)

Counselors must operate in boundary terms in a manner that enables them to move across the counselor-client interpersonal line — for identification purposes — but at the same time they must remain firmly anchored within their own boundary space — for objectivity purposes.

— Gary Hermansson (1997)

On the surface, the issue of maintaining appropriate boundaries seems cut and dried: avoid physical intimacies and dual relationships with clients, maintain an appropriate emotional distance, and establish clear limits on client contact outside of therapy. However, boundary dilemmas are not always limited to inappropriate actions. Sometimes difficulties arise when we become so overwhelmed with the client's struggles that empathy gives rise to symbiosis. We must be on guard for such cases: the adult survivor of child or physical abuse, the betrayed spouse, the grieving parent, the physically disabled. Sometimes we over-identify or fuse with clients because of our own histories and vulnerabilities — their pain becomes our pain.

On the other hand, some clinicians may distance themselves emotionally to protect themselves from their feelings. In either case, we may be unable to maintain a professional and productive focus. Sometimes, as in the following scenario, the boundary issue involves whether to cross traditional lines in the service of a therapeutic goal.

❖ A Case in Point

Arnold Lazarus, in his book *Brief But Comprehensive Psychotherapy* (1997), describes the case of a successful stockbroker, Lance, aged thirty-five, whose real forte was self-criticism. He believed that he "should have accomplished more, should be tackling new challenges." This negative pattern resulted in a poor self-image in spite of his accomplishments. To counter his lack of confidence, Lazarus emphasized a "peer" approach in therapy, utilizing collaboration and reliance on Lance's strengths and problem-solving skills. After several months, Lance invited the therapist and his wife to dinner. Apparently the treatment was working so well that the client had taken seriously the notion that he and his therapist were peers. This put the clinician in a tough spot — refuse the invitation and risk Lance feeling misled about his worth or violate conventional boundary limits. In this case, the therapist decided that the client's well-being outweighed a rigid acceptance of the admonition against boundary crossing.

❖ Putting It into Practice

Take immediate action when the client seems to be engaging in boundary-crossing behaviors, such as excessive phone calls or other attempts for out-of-session contact. There is a tendency for therapists to take a "wait and see" attitude when it comes to such issues: "If I don't say anything, maybe the behavior will go away." This is simply wishful thinking, or denial, depending on your school of thought. The reality is that ignoring the problem is likely to make it worse — once a boundary line is crossed, the tendency is for clients to push the boundaries even further.

> *We all have our favored ways of making uncomfortable ethical challenges disappear, perhaps by transforming them, almost magically, into something else, perhaps by attacking the client or colleague who raises the ethical question, perhaps by viewing ourselves as helpless.*
>
> — Kenneth Pope and Melba Vasquez (1998)

Remind yourself that the greatest number of complaints to boards of psychology involve therapist violations of physical intimacy regulations. The temptation to violate this fundamental ethical precept can be all too great when therapists do not meet their own relationship and romantic needs outside of their clinical practice.

> *Malpractice suits against therapists for sexual misconduct are skyrocketing.... It is easy to see how it could happen in light of the fact that 87 percent of practicing therapists admit to feeling sexually attracted to their clients.*
>
> — Jeffrey Kottler (2003)

Maintaining emotional boundaries is as important as maintaining physical boundaries. Therapists must continually strive to avoid overidentification or "fusion" with their clients.

> *Some of us take empathy to an unhealthy extreme where we not only understand our patient's pain, we "feel their pain." This leaves us vulnerable to emotional burnout and renders us less objective and effective in our efforts to heal.*
>
> — Michelle Webster (1991)

❖ *Therapy and Men*

For men, psychotherapy is the antithesis of "masculinity." To enter therapy a man must violate several tenets of the credo of "manhood."

— Richard Meth et al. (2006)

We have come to the conclusion that therapists often fail to recognize core male needs. . . . Men are being told that their natural mode of communication is unacceptable despite the fact that biologically and socially they have not been equipped to share complex and confusing feelings as easily as are women. When men hear. . . messages like this in therapy, they do not expect to be either liked or understood.

— Paul Gilbert (2000)

Fathers rarely make the call to set up a first appointment. However, they frequently make the call to cancel a session.

— Berthold Berg and Neil Rosenblum (1977)

All clients present challenges in one way or another. However, working with men can be particularly challenging in that they will often see the therapeutic process itself as something foreign to the male psyche: submitting to the authority of a stranger, disclosing failings and insecurities, revealing family and personal secrets. No wonder women make up 70 to 80 percent of the client population both in inpatient and outpatient settings (Chin et al, 2003). Marital counseling (often called marital "canceling" because of the frequency of missed sessions) is even a more torturous experience in which men are subjected to a litany of complaints such as not sharing intimate feelings, caring only about sex, enjoying his friends more than his family, and not sharing in parenting responsibilities. And yet, a number of studies show that increasing numbers of men report that family and marital relationships are the most important things in their lives (Gray, 2002).

So wherein lies the truth? Do men crave emotional closeness or are they genetically and culturally programmed to avoid commitment and emotional expression? Are they willing to discuss their personal struggles and rely on an "expert's" guidance? What can we do as clinicians to engage them in the therapeutic process?

❖ A Case in Point

Armando was the quintessential man who could not listen to his wife's concerns without trying to problem-solve when what she really needed was some empathy. The idea of just being supportive went so against Armando's masculine grain that his wife would no longer confide in him, leaving both parties frustrated. The solution was simple enough: teach Armando to not problem-solve and to listen just as a friend would. Two therapists later, the problem remained unsolved. What to do? The third therapist reviewed what had failed in the previous therapy and decided that rather than hit a brick wall again, the goal would be to have Armando solve a different but related problem; that is, he was to identify the emotional state his wife was in and try to do something about that, not the content of the problem. Thus, if she seemed anxious, he would urge her to take a few deep breaths, if sad, he would console her by holding her hand. Armando received this solution positively because it recognized his need to problem-solve rather than trying to "correct" something that to him was a natural mode of responding.

❖ Putting It into Practice

Acknowledge that many men feel awkward and guilty about entering into therapy.

Let your male clients know that the act of seeking help when needed is both an act of courage and maturity — particularly when one feels anxious and resistant about doing so.

> — Olga Silverstein and Beth Rashbaum (1995)

Avoid the "touchy feely" approach early in therapy.

Bite your tongue if you find yourself about to ask the hallmark question of all therapeutic work: "And how did that make you feel?"

> — Alon Gratch (2006)

Concentrate on active strategies that provide the male client with a sense of control and direction.

Remember the dropout rate is high for clients in general, and more so for the male client. Thus early sessions should focus on achievable and collaborative goals, out of session activities, lists and diagrams and perhaps behavior change contracts.

— Terrence Real (1998)

Acknowledge the effectiveness of certain workplace strategies while developing alternative approaches to handle family matters. Because men are often resistant to attending therapy in the first place, it is especially important when attempting to modify behaviors for clinicians to avoid what men may construe as criticism or negativity.

When investigating a client's tendency to utilize a "take charge" attitude at home to deal with family matters, it can be pointed out that this has been a useful and productive strategy in the workplace, which has helped the client achieve a good deal of success. Following such a supportive statement, the therapist can then clarify that a strategy which works well in one venue may be counterproductive in another such as the family milieu.

— Richard Meth et al. (2006)

❖ *Therapy and Women*

Confusing and poorly conceived communications from mothers are the primary toxic agent in schizophrenia.

— William Goldfarb et al. (1996)

Infertility is a psychosomatic defense which can be interpreted as the woman's unconscious anxiety about motherhood.

— Leon Chertok et al. (1963)

In taking up a masculine calling, studying and working in man's way, woman is doing something not wholly in agreement, if not directly injurious to her feminine nature.

— Carl Jung (1999)

As the preceding quotations make clear, since the inception of psychotherapy, bias and ignorance have permeated the way clinicians have diagnosed and treated women. Therapists saw women as responsible for their reproductive difficulties; blamed them for a wide variety of their children's problems, from asthma to schizophrenia to autism, and saw them as deviant if they aspired to more than the maternal and homemaker roles. Fortunately, we live in more enlightened times — times in which the majority of graduate psychology students are, in fact, women (Chin, 2003). However, we are still challenged to understand our female clients' struggles from a broader perspective, rather than merely assigning them to traditional diagnostic categories.

❖ A Case in Point

A therapist sensitive to women's issues encountered a woman struggling through a divorce while parenting three young children, having few financial resources. Rather than label her as "depressed," they invoked the term "The Exhaustion." A change in vocabulary indicates a change in consciousness. Using such a term makes it far more likely that economic and gender relations will become an acknowledged part of the conversation . . . and perhaps the realms of action will include seeking both relief and redress.

— Shona Russell and Maggie Carey (2004)

❖ Putting It into Practice

Understand the sociocultural underpinnings of disorders with which women clients present. We can address eating disorders, battered wife syndrome, and lack of assertiveness most effectively within a substantial psychoeducational component aimed at "consciousness raising."

For example, anorexics and bulimics need to appreciate our society's obsession with the idea that one can "never be too thin," and how that obsession permeates young girls' lives from Barbie dolls in childhood to teen magazines which emphasize attaining the "body beautiful" to impossibly thin mannequins in department stores, to fashion models on starvation diets.

— Harriet Lerner (1989)

Recognize that there are certain situations in which a woman client would be best matched with a woman clinician.

It is a blatant paradox and therefore often ineffective for male therapists to attempt to "empower" female clients to be more assertive in their relationships with men.

— Miriam Greenspan (1993)

Understand the emotional conundrum caused by the conflict many women experience when trying to meet both maternal and occupational needs.

Those fighting for women's progress too often misconstrue the maternal role as a throwback or excuse, a self-curtailment of potential. Those who champion the role too often define it narrowly in the context of service — to one's child, husband or God. What each view eclipses is the authentic desire to mother felt by a woman herself — a desire not derived by a child's need; a desire not created by a social role; rather a desire anchored in herself as an agent, as an autonomous individual, a person.

— Daphne de Marneffe (2004)

❖ *Accepting Our Clinical Limitations*

Acknowledge your limitations or they will tyrannize over you.

— Mason Cooley (1996)

Read through your case files. What clients do you seem to hold onto while others fall away after a few sessions? How flexible is your style and approach? What developmental issues of your own ... are reflected in your work?

— Robert Taibbi (1996)

Restraining our egos is a challenge that many of us will never quite meet. What with our diplomas, titles, and carefully appointed chambers, it is hard for us not to take ourselves too seriously.

— Jeffrey Kottler (2003)

You would think that once a person reaches the pinnacle in his or her particular field, it would be time to breathe a sigh of relief, ease up, enjoy the view. But the fact is those who make it to number one often work even harder than before so they can remain on top. An example of this is Roger Federer, currently ranked the top tennis player in the world. After a 2006 tournament, when a TV interviewer asked about his plans, he responded that he still needed to work on a couple of aspects of his game that were weak.

Although as therapists we don't have rankings, we can reach a place where we think we pretty much have seen it all, heard it all, read it all. As our caseload expands, our egos may do so as well. We may feel that we are infallible. Thus, if clients drop out or complain about a lack of progress, we might "shoot the messenger," chalking it up to the client's resistance or unwillingness to change. Recognizing our fallibility allows us to consider the possibility that the client may need another perspective; that is, it may be time to consult or refer.

Such actions require we swallow our professional pride, which can be a bitter pill.

❖ A Case in Point

Eight-year-old Daniel and his ten-year-old brother David had not seen their biological father in five years, following an acrimonious divorce. During that time their father had been working overseas, but upon his return he wished to resume visitations with his children. Their mother and stepfather were adamantly opposed to this — and in fact had told the children that they would never have to see their father again. The court, however, had a different idea and stated that the children should be helped by a therapist to reunite with their father. The lawyers referred the case to me (J.F.), and it was my job to prepare the children for a first visit. Daniel was quite willing to give his biological father a chance, but David was so anxious and resistant that he would not even discuss the matter with me. After a few sessions of trying everything to reduce David's anxiety and gain his confidence, I finally recognized that I was not making the necessary connection with him. Hard as it was on the ego, I decided that perhaps a different therapist, ideally a woman, would be best in this case, and I made the appropriate (and ultimately more successful) referral.

❖ Putting It into Practice

Recognize that needing to refer a client is not equivalent to having failed as a therapist.

The difference between genius and stupidity is that genius has its limits.

— Albert Einstein (2005)

Avoid unrealistic expectations and goals as a therapist.

You are not going to cure schizophrenia... or wipe out chronic depression by disputing a few irrational beliefs.

— Jeffrey Kottler (2003)

Understand that being appreciated for "curing" our clients is less important than doing what is necessary to help them.

Like all human beings, we crave reinforcement for our actions. However, the drive to receive our client's gratitude can get in the way of our making an appropriate referral. Our job as therapists is not about "ego-stroking." It is about helping clients get on with their lives — and then forgetting about us.

— Donald Meichenbaum (2005)

On the Nature of the Healing Relationship

There is a logic to human relationships wherein a single new relationship or a changed older one can reverberate throughout the individual's entire psychic system and change the entire internal system of meanings about the self, the self in relation to others and/or even attributions about the goodness or badness of life in general.

— C. Everett Bailey (2005)

Is doing therapy an "art" or a "science"? Or is it both? Like medical practitioners, mental health clinicians assess, diagnose, and develop treatment plans. However, there are significant differences between the medical and therapy models. The most important of these is that effective therapy relies more heavily on relationship factors as a curative force. In fact, the specific interventions that therapists apply are less predictive of positive therapy outcomes than is the quality of the therapist-client relationship. At the heart of that relationship is the sense that the therapist cares about the client. This caring is expressed continuously throughout the therapeutic endeavor, manifesting at various times as empathy, patience, forgiveness, encouragement, and firm but concerned confrontation. Above all else, healers communicate clearly and listen carefully and deeply to their clients.

❖ *Bonding*

How well medications serve their intended purpose has been shown to be partly a result of the relationship between the drug giver and the drug receiver. Learning in school has been demonstrated to depend in part on the teacher-pupil relationship. The subject's behavior in the experimental laboratory can be readily influenced by the experimenter-subject relationship.

— Frederick Kanfer and Arnold Goldstein (1980)

It is imperative that clinicians remember that decades of research consistently demonstrate that relationship factors correlate more highly with client outcome than do specialized treatment techniques.

— Louis Castonguay et al. (1996)

Bonding seems to make possible a greater sense of self-esteem in the client, providing the client with an enhanced capacity for carrying out life's tasks.

— Mo Therese Hannah (2005)

Those who have worked in the educational field are familiar with the interesting explanations students provide for having done poorly in a course. One rarely hears that the course was too hard or that the student didn't put forth enough effort. What the student often says, rather, is something akin to "I didn't like the instructor." It is intriguing that students would rather punish themselves with a poor grade than give their disliked instructor the pleasure of thinking they had learned something.

For clinicians, there is a tremendous lesson here that much clinical research validates: a weak bond predicts a weak effort on the part of the client, whereas a strong bond is central in motivating the client to undertake corrective actions and cognitive change (Greenberg & Horvath, 1989). No other single factor affects therapy outcome more than the quality of the client-therapist relationship. Edward Bordin, who pioneered research on the "working alliance," put it this way: "The bond . . . is the vehicle that enables and facilitates the specific counseling techniques employed by the clinician" (Bordin, 1994). Techniques, though useful, are insufficient by themselves.

❖ A Case in Point

Adrian was the poster child of a graduate psychology student. He rarely did less than perfectly on papers and exams, and he had published several professional-level research papers by the time he graduated. But when he started practicing, one small problem arose — his client dropout rate was nearly as high as his grades had been. This was not a case of not being adroit at diagnosis and treatment planning; he knew what to do and how to do it.

Adrian would have been a great therapist — if it hadn't been for the clients. He just didn't know how to connect with them. Reviewing Adrian's taped sessions, his supervisors determined that he approached therapy as if it were analogous to repairing an automobile — tell the customers (clients) what the problem is, what needs to be done to fix it, and when it will be finished. The human element was missing. For Adrian there was never any time for chitchat, for asking about how the client's favorite team did that week, where they were going to spend their upcoming vacation, or whether the kids had recovered from the flu. Instead it was "How did the homework assignment go?" "On a scale from zero to ten, where is the depression this week?" These are relevant questions but not the stuff of which bonds are made.

❖ Putting It into Practice

Treat each session as an opportunity to strengthen the bond between therapist and client.

Warmly welcome the client — making eye contact, shaking hands and perhaps offering a beverage. All too often therapists wave in the next client much as an accountant does so at tax time — "next victim?"

— Eve Lipchik (2002)

Ask clients periodically if they feel understood and respected.

Because I have heard clients say that they felt hurt or disrespected if people were too curt with them . . . like they are not interested, I always ask them early on if they feel respected and understood by me.

— Len Jennings (2005)

Voice your admiration for demonstrations of client strengths, survival skills, and personality characteristics.

Remind yourself that clients are more than their problems. Every client has resources that can be tapped to further therapeutic progress.

— Milton Erickson et al. (1982)

Do not take the therapist-client relationship for granted.

Like all relationships the therapeutic one can have its ups and downs. Be mindful of changes in the amount of warmth and energy that the client is expressing session by session, and gently inquire if you suspect a change in the nature of the bond.

— Leslie Greenberg and Susan Johnson (1988)

 ## *Caring*

There have been some medical schools… in which somewhere along the assembly line, a faculty member has informed the students, not so much by what he said but by what he did, that there is an intimate relation between curing and caring.

— Ashley Montagu (1988)

The Cycle of Caring — of Empathetic Attachment, Active Involvement, and Felt Separation — describes the continual relational process that summarizes the work of the counselor.

— Thomas Skovholt and Len Jennings (2005)

Caring is the human mode of being. One becomes authentically human as one's capacity to care is called forth, nurtured and expressed.

— M. Simone Roach (1997)

One of the most important factors in a strong therapist-client bond is the therapist's ability to clearly convey a sense of caring. This process begins with the very first greeting and continues throughout therapy until termination and even beyond. We convey it in words and in ways beyond words. One of the most insightful studies of therapist behavior involved asking clients to describe moments or actions that were particularly helpful during the course of therapy. Some of the most common responses involved times when the therapist did something simple to express caring — offering a cup of coffee, leaning toward the client during the session, making regular eye contact, walking the client to the door — all little acts of caring (Egan, 1998).

❖ A Case in Point

The noted clinician Michael Mahoney describes in his book, *Constructive Psychotherapy*, that he had been invited to deliver a presentation on the essential ingredients of effective therapy. He was working on the speech when a client arrived for her appointment. He left the room for a few minutes to fetch her a soda, and upon his return he noticed she was perusing the outline of his speech, which he had left on his desk. "What do you think about the speech?" he asked. "Where's the caring?" she replied. "What do you mean?" said Dr. Mahoney. "Well, your outline talks about many things, but you left out the most important thing that you have done for me — you showed me that you really care (Mahoney, 2005).

❖ Putting It into Practice

Convey to clients that their struggles, successes, and setbacks matter to you — that their well-being is a deep concern, not just as a professional, but on a personal level as well.

I work hard to communicate to my basketball players that above all, I am their biggest fan — that I am rooting for them to succeed.

— John Wooden (2001)

Do not confuse "caring about" your clients with "taking care of" them.

In caring to help a person grow, I experience what I care for as an extension of myself, and at the same time as something separate from me that I respect individually. Instead of trying to dominate and possess others . . . I want them to grow in their own right.

— Milton Meyeroff (1971)

Consider that with depressed and suicidal clients, caring becomes doubly important and doubly complex.

In such cases, we must provide a nonjudgmental and supportive atmosphere in which the client can tell his or her story — including negative and suicidal thoughts, images, feelings and behaviors.

— Donald Meichenbaum (2005)

❖ *Empathy*

It is the experience of touching the pain of others that is the key to change.

— Jim Wallis (2005)

It is only when I understand the thoughts that seem so horrible to you, or so weak, or so sentimental, or so bizarre, it is only as I see them as you see them, that you feel free . . . to explore your inner and often buried experience.

— Carl Rogers (1961)

Patients who felt that their therapy was successful described their therapist as "warm, attentive, interested, understanding, and respectful."

— Hans Strupp and Anne Bloxom (1973)

We cannot and need not actually "feel the pain" of our clients to display our empathy: our intimate understanding of their thoughts, feelings, and motivations. However, through attentiveness and genuine concern, we can create a harmonic connection — an echo — that signifies: "I understand, and you are not alone in this experience." Little wonder that dozens of studies have identified numerous benefits resulting from therapist empathy (Greenberg, Watson & Elliot, 2001). These include increased client satisfaction, enhanced feelings of safety, and greater retention in therapy. And that is just the beginning. Empathy has been found to help clients think more productively; it facilitates emotional reprocessing; and, finally, it helps therapists choose interventions compatible with the client's frame of reference.

Nearly every graduate student of psychology has memorized Carl Rogers's three cornerstones of therapeutic work: unconditional positive regard, therapist congruence or authenticity, and empathic understanding. However, one of the most common reasons clients give for leaving therapy prematurely is not feeling understood. What happened to all that training in reading clients' feelings? Heaven knows we ask them "How does that feel?" often enough! Perhaps too often we become a slave to protocol — make the diagnosis, develop the treatment plan, state the measurable goals, report to the HMO — and somewhere we forget the human being we are treating.

❖ A Case in Point

After thoroughly assessing and diagnosing Shantell with stress-related health problems, Dr. Jordan developed a comprehensive treatment plan involving stress reduction techniques, dietary change, exercise . . . everything but the kitchen sink. Much to her surprise, Shantell looked less than enthusiastic.

"Is there something you would like to tell me?" Dr. Jordan queried. "Yes," Shantell responded, "You really know your stuff about stress and health. It's just that it seems like you have done this so often that it's like you're doing it by rote — and I don't feel you know *me* very well yet." Turns out, Shantell knew all about stress reduction; the problem was a different one entirely: she had lost hope. She feared that her health had deteriorated so much it was useless to undertake any remedial steps. Having found the "real" issue, Dr. Jordan developed a completely different treatment protocol.

❖ Putting It into Practice

Allow clients to talk about their feelings about therapy before entering into the "core" issues that have brought them to seek help.

Initially, I ask questions such as: "Is this your first experience with therapy?" If so, then I might follow up by saying: "That can be uncomfortable" or "It can be hard to come to a stranger to talk about things that are troublesome."

— Mary Pipher (2003)

Recognize how being unable to resolve personal difficulties without help from others can diminish one's self-esteem.

Most clients enter therapy feeling vulnerable and helpless. They feel a lack of control over their lives . . . and fear judgment and the unknown.

— Claude Villenueve (2001)

Recognize that clients are often quite anxious about making changes in their lives, even when they perceive those changes as necessary.

When I find evidence of such anxiety... I empathize by normalizing it and help clients accept rather than fight the feelings... I tell them that the anxiety may actually serve a good purpose because it is telling you to slow down in order to get used to the changes that are possible.

— Eve Lipchik (2002)

When dealing with clients whose behavior appears hypocritical, be sensitive to the difficulty of the human condition and the tendency to avoid or deny moral inconsistencies.

The client who says he cherishes "family values" while having an extra-marital affair; the animal rights activist who eats meat; the student who cheats on exams but will no longer talk to a friend who betrayed a secret — such cases challenge therapists to avoid condemnation — while helping the client explore whether their behaviors are the best solutions.

— Charles Batson et al. (1999)

❖ *Acceptance*

Unconditional positive regard involves a feeling of acceptance for the client's expression of negative, "bad," painful, fearful, defensive, abnormal feelings as for his expression of "good," positive, mature, confident, social feelings.

— Carl Rogers (1961)

Unconditional acceptance and caring are a critical part of the relationship between the therapist and the client. This does not mean that the therapist likes everything about the client or that every behavior is encouraged.

— John Gartner (2000)

Change is the brother of acceptance, but it is the younger brother.

— Andrew Christensen and Neil Jacobson (1998)

"Be accepting of your clients." Who can argue with that? But what exactly constitutes acceptance? Acceptance does not mean sitting by passively, exhibiting a Buddha-like serene indifference while our clients repeatedly engage in behavior that is detrimental to themselves or others. Rather, acceptance is active:

❖ It means accepting clients as they are at present, coupled with the belief that they are "helpable," that with time, support, and guidance change is possible.

❖ It means exploring the clients' background to shed light on the source and power of their negative patterns — not to justify or seek blame, but to broaden the perspective.

❖ It means trying to connect with the person behind the negative behaviors or attitudes, recognizing that their acts are not the totality of who they are and that no matter what their attitudes or actions, their "personhood" also includes their strengths and their accomplishments.

❖ A Case in Point

Keiko had done the unthinkable. Following a drunken argument with her fourth husband, she had intimate relations with her fourteen-year-old son. The police charged her, and her lawyer referred her for evaluation and treatment prior to her trial.

OK, let's practice acceptance. But how? When a person violates the paramount tenet of parenting — to protect one's child — the ability to be accepting is tested to the limit. To work effectively with the client in this case, the therapist needed to be gently honest that this was a difficult case for him because of the nature of the act. Fortunately, Keiko understood and accepted this and she seemed to reflect honestly on the need to repair her relationship with her son, seek marital counseling, and get help for her alcohol problem. Her commitment to change enhanced the therapist's ability to work with her and he came to see her act as an aberrant action that she would not repeat.

❖ Putting It into Practice

Being accepting is no easy thing. It requires accepting the good, bad, and ugly of the client's emotional life and attitudes toward the therapist.

Can I really allow the client to feel hostile toward me?... Can I accept when the client views life and its problems in a way quite different from mine?... Can I accept him when he feels very positively towards me, and wants to model himself after me?

— Carl Rogers (1961)

Your expression of acceptance of clients both increases the therapeutic bond and is a means to therapeutic ends.

Acceptance of the client by the therapist leads to an increased acceptance of the self by the client.

— John Bradshaw (1988)

Remember that there is significant evidence that lack of self-acceptance is at the root of many emotional difficulties (Bongers, de Winter, & Kompier, 1993; Boyd, 2002; Kadushin, 1996).

Laboratory studies have shown that rejected participants are less likely to act in prosocial ways; they exhibit an assortment of cognitive deficits such as impaired logical reasoning, a distorted time perception, and an emphasis on the present rather than the future. They also exhibit self-destructive tendencies . . . such as foolish risk taking and unhealthy choices.

— Roy Baumeister et al. (2005)

❖ *Trustworthiness*

Therapy is founded not on esoteric concepts but on concrete, living moments that are the bedrock from which truth and trust evolve. How a person has been addressed or dismissed, heard or silenced, acknowledged or discredited, constitutes the cornerstone of his or her wholeness, uniqueness and courage to face the world.

— Barbara Krasner and Austin Joyce (1995)

There is a great difference, then, between "power" and "authority." Power refers to one's ability to coerce others. . . . Authority must be performed. Authority refers to one's ability to gain trust.

— Joel Meyerwitz (1998)

If therapists aren't willing to strive for genuine sincerity, despite all the attendant risks and possible complications, then they deny their patients the opportunity of working through the difficulties of achieving sincerity in any human relationship. Moments of true mutual sincerity in psychotherapy are healing not only because of the insight achieved but also because they restore the damaged hope that sincerity is possible.

— Ron Morstyn (2002)

When clients are asked to look back at the course of their therapy and to report what has helped them most, they often refer to specific statements that stuck with them — a bit of wisdom, encouragement, or constructive criticism that provided guidance at a pivotal moment. For our words to have that kind of lasting power, we must endeavor to build and maintain our client's trust that we will say what we mean and mean what we say.

Perhaps a therapist's worst nightmare is to have a client question our sincerity: "Did you really mean it when you said I am making progress?" "Are you really glad that my boyfriend and I made up?" "Do you really understand how attached I was to my dog?" To ask such questions is really to ask: "Can I trust you? Are there genuine feelings and facts behind your words of concern, praise, or approval — or just politeness?" Another facet of the trusting relationship involves the client's sense of safety with the therapist — the safety that permits accepting guidance and interventions that may seem risky. Implementing even a seemingly benign technique such as relaxation training requires a high level of trust in the therapist, as the following case history demonstrates.

❖ A Case in Point

Candace had been a star player on the college soccer team her first season, but in her second year her performance deteriorated significantly. Her coach referred her to a campus therapist, and Candace confided that her main problem involved her mother's heavy drinking and daily verbal abuse. She stated that she was having great difficulty sleeping and concentrating and that she felt on the verge of a nervous breakdown.

Relaxation training seemed to be a reasonable first step. However, shortly after beginning the procedure, the client became visibly uncomfortable and asked the therapist if she was trying to hypnotize her. The therapist reassured Candace that she was not using hypnosis and that if she was uncomfortable they could try relaxation another time. However, apparently the damage had been done. Candace did not return for further counseling.

❖ Putting It into Practice

Recognize that the underpinning of the therapist-client relationship, regardless of theoretical orientation, is trust.

Clients must trust that we are committed to helping them without hurting them ... this means getting clients to trust us to help them trust themselves.

— Eve Lipchik (2002)

Understand that trustworthiness is not an abstract concept but one that our actions and reactions continually make manifest.

Trust involves telling it like it is. It means when a client notices that you look bored, admitting that you are (if you are) and discussing why that might be; it means that when a client asks if you support a course of action they have decided on — that you think is a bad choice — you tell them so; it means when clients ask if they are getting better, supporting their progress, while pointing out avenues that can lead to even greater progress.

— John Norcross (2002)

Avoid challenging clients' religious, political, or other deeply held values. How can they trust us to help them if they believe that our entire worldview and theirs are in conflict?

There is a difference between clarifying a client's religious beliefs in order to more fully understand their beliefs — and challenging them — the former can be illuminating, the latter can destroy trust in the therapist.

— William Sabine and Gail Steketee (2006)

❖ *Responsiveness to Negative Feedback*

Few people have the wisdom to prefer the criticism that would do them good, to the praise that deceives them.

— François de La Rochefoucauld (1665-1678)

An empathic lapse occurs when the therapist misunderstands the patient. If the lapse is not acknowledged by the therapist, the treatment may suffer. If the incident is recognized and discussed, the relationship and the treatment may be revitalized.

— Suzanne Bender and Edward Messner (2003)

Coaches have to watch for what they don't want to see, and listen for what they don't want to hear.

— John Madden (1984)

No matter how hard therapists try to be helpful, supportive, and attentive, inevitably there will be times when clients feel insulted, neglected, misunderstood, or disappointed in their therapeutic progress — exactly the opposite of what we hope and strive for. When clients voice their concerns, it is actually a sign of courage and trust in the relationship. It is a chance for us to recognize this courage and to honestly evaluate the clients' reflections. Unfortunately, all too often therapists "shoot the messenger," that is, they respond defensively to negative client feedback, labeling it as either transference or distorted thinking, depending on the clinician's orientation. This kind of response can do great damage to the therapeutic relationship, creating a rupture in which clients feel "not heard" and belittled for honestly expressing their concerns.

❖ Cases in Point

Even someone as omni-successful and highly respected as Oprah Winfrey is not immune to the tendency to self-protect and shift the blame elsewhere when accused of impropriety. Initially, Oprah rose to the defense of author James Frey, who was found to have fabricated several significant portions of his memoir on addiction recovery. She took the position that the book's essence was what mattered most, not specific details. After reflection, however (and a good deal of negative press), she decided to devote an entire show to the matter. On television, in front of millions, she admitted not only that Frey duped her, but also that she was mistaken when she implied that the truth of the book was less important than the message it provided. Even though Oprah believed that it was the "only appropriate option for her to take," it was still an act of extreme courage, repairing the breach in the public's trust of her (Winfrey, 2006).

After a long day with clients, Dr Singh's final client, nineteen-year-old Kasey, arrived and launched into her usual tirade against her parents, teachers, brother, and the family pet. At one point, Dr. Singh tried hard to stifle a yawn, but there was no escaping Kasey's vigilance. "Am I boring you?" she queried straightforwardly. The therapist, like a deer caught in the headlights, was first taken aback and began to disavow any hint of lack of interest. Realizing there was no escape, Dr. Singh changed course mid-sentence and owned up to the fact that they seemed to be revisiting the same complaints as before and wondered if it wouldn't be more productive to move on to other matters. Kasey wasn't thrilled with the response, but it did prod her to recognize her tendency to focus too much on negative patterns within her family. More important, she felt validated in voicing her concerns about the therapist's behavior.

❖ Putting It into Practice

Periodically allow for client feedback on the progress of therapy.

It is also the therapist's job to accept and use the patient's feedback and observations of the therapist's impact on the therapy.

— John Norcross (2002)

Use difficulties in the therapist-client relationship as a model of conflict resolution that the client can apply in the real world.

A therapy relationship is like all other relationships... and how we repair the rupture in our relationship can also help with ruptures occurring in other relationships.

— Thomas Skovholt and Len Jennings (2005)

Recognize the powerful relationship between eliciting client feedback (both positive and negative) and therapeutic outcome.

Perhaps contrary to expectations, those clients who were given opportunities to provide feedback to therapists had higher rates of attendance and more positive therapy outcomes.

— Jason Whipple et al. (2003)

On the Characteristics
of Healers

[When] clients enter a therapist's office, they will more likely look for indications of who the therapist is rather than for a particular diploma on the wall. Personal authenticity, genuine respect, and concern for the client are more essential.

— Monica McGoldrick et al. (1996)

The master therapist, teacher, coach and mentor all share the ability to flexibly embrace complex ambiguity, accumulate wisdom, understand the human condition, and make learning a lifelong adventure.

— Thomas Skovholt and Len Jennings (2005)

A healer's actions ultimately reflect who that healer is as a person. The inner qualities that give rise to healing behaviors include emotional intelligence (EI), passion, patience, creativity, and flexibility. In addition, there is the deep-seated drive to assist, to empower, to encourage, and to support. The healer also places a high value on ethics and, thus, does not betray the trust of her or his clients, avoids exploitation of any kind, and does not feel the need to diminish others to feel a relative sense of power. Lastly, therapists who heal are open to change and willing to tolerate ambiguity, as growth often depends on leaving the familiar and entering unknown territory.

❖ *Emotional Intelligence*

Emotionally intelligent individuals know how to express themselves, at the right level, at the right time, while ideally striving to enhance long-term goals versus achieving the sometimes reckless satisfaction of an immediate emotional reaction.

— Daniel Goleman (1995)

Expecting to ride through life on the coattails of a high IQ alone is like expecting to be handed your first driver's license after only a written test. IQ predicts only how we'll do on paper. . . EQ (emotional IQ) illuminates our inner world.

— Jeanne Segal (1997)

I am indeed a king because I know how to rule myself.

— Pietro Aretino (1492-1556)

We all know people with average intelligence who have nonetheless achieved a very high level of success. Frequently, their accomplishments are the result of their highly developed people skills — the ability to read others well and to connect with them at a personal level. What they might lack in skills or talents, they make up for with passion, warmth, and self-awareness. These qualities serve people well in many fields, including the political and corporate realms, but in the therapeutic setting, they are indispensable. Emotionally intelligent therapists know how to calm themselves and their clients. They know when to push and when to console. They know how to avoid succumbing to the contagion of the client's anger, sadness, or anxiety. They anticipate their client's reactions and tune in to verbal and nonverbal signals. They are a pleasure to be around.

Although there are abundant definitions of EI, all seem to share these four increasingly complex skills:

1. Perceiving emotions. High EI people can identify a variety of feelings in themselves and others. They are also adept at recognizing emotions portrayed in stories, art, and music.
2. Using emotions. This means being able to harness emotions to solve problems, make decisions, and communicate interpersonally.

3. Understanding emotions. This skill includes recognizing the circumstances under which certain emotions arise and recognizing how two or more emotions can operate simultaneously.
4. Managing emotions. This complex ability involves the ability to reduce or enhance an emotional response in oneself and others as well as the ability to experience a range of emotions while making decisions about the appropriateness or usefulness of the emotion in a given situation.

❖ A Case in Point

Crystal is a generally pleasant and well-behaved twelve-year-old. Pleasant, that is, until she and her younger brother start picking on each other. Often this needling reaches its height at the dinner table where they trade insults and make faces at one another. On one such occasion, her brother made a disparaging remark about her weight and this pushed Crystal to her emotional limits. However, instead of blowing up, she calmly stood and stated, "I think I need a timeout," and she exited the room. A few minutes later she returned, having regained her composure, and asked her brother if he had matured any while she was gone.

Crystal belongs to a family where the parents help the children to notice when their emotions are getting the best of them. They teach them how to regain self-control through such methods as distraction, humor, or, if need be, taking a short timeout. At twelve, Crystal has internalized these skills and can use them on her own, without her parents' prompting. Unfortunately many of us, therapists included, come from homes that are "emotionally impoverished," and thus we must make special efforts to develop our EQs to best serve our clients.

❖ Putting It into Practice

Enhance your "perceiving emotions" skills by practicing reading the emotions of characters in movies or people being interviewed on television talk shows or newscasts. When watching films at home, for instance, turn off the sound and try to discern the actors' emotions from their nonverbal language.

Responsive parents [and effective therapists] are attuned to a person's emotional signals, such as body language, facial expression, tone of voice, and energy level.

— Mary Ainsworth and John Bowlby (1953)

Take stock of the strategies that you employ to manage your own strong emotions. As therapists, we often train our clients in emotional regulation but neglect to use it in our own lives.

Venting, problem-solving, positive self-talk and self-soothing are some of the tools by which we manage our emotions, instead of being enslaved by them.

— Marcia Hughes et al. (2005)

Investigate your EI using self-assessment instruments such as the EQ-i (Dawda & Hart, 2000) or the EQ Map (Khanna & Vohra, 2000). These assessment tools provide insight into areas of strengths as well as components of the EQ that could profit from development.

Self-awareness is the doorway to emotional intelligence, and by opening the door (through self-assessment) you will instantly gain useful insights into yourself.

— Adele Lynn (2004)

❖ *Passion*

I want to be thoroughly used up when I die, for the harder I work the more I live. I rejoice in life for its own sake. Life is no "brief candle" to me. It is a sort of splendid torch which I have got hold of for the moment, and I want to make it burn as brightly as possible before handing it on to future generations.

— George Bernard Shaw (1903)

Passionately committed psychotherapists are defined as those who maintain an enthusiasm for their work regardless of time on the job, and for whom work produces more energy than it demands.

— Raymond Dlugos and Myrna Friedlander (2001)

Those who honor their passions rarely get stuck in who they are now. Instead they begin to blossom into who they might be.

— Sam Keen (1992)

George Allen, the longtime NFL and USFL coach, once said, "If you hate your job, don't worry, you won't have it long" (1989). The message is that even if a person can tolerate doing work that is distasteful, ultimately one's performance is bound to suffer, and this will not go unnoticed. The opposite is also true. People who bring passion to their work energize themselves and those with whom they come in contact. Of course we cannot manufacture passion, but we can remind ourselves daily of the joy and challenge that doing clinical work provides. Getting pumped up for clients hour after hour day after day is a challenge.

One therapist, Bradford Keeney, in his book *Improvisation Therapy*, has developed a number of approaches for therapists to "keep it new." As a sports enthusiast, he has utilized the idea of the "batter's box" in baseball. He recommends that before each client enters the office the clinician stand as if she is about to face a pitcher in a pivotal moment in a game. Take a couple of practice swings. Shift your feet to get just the right stance (2005). If baseball isn't your thing, perhaps imagining yourself being introduced to give a speech before a large audience or a simple moment of quiet reflection can help set the stage for greeting the next client with a greater sense of energy and focus.

❖ Putting It into Practice

Select continuing education courses that renew, revitalize, and challenge your theoretical base — not just those that are convenient and fit with your school of thought.

Isn't success just loving your life and working with the same degree of passion?

— Lawler Kang and Mark Albion (2005)

If you have developed a clinical niche or specialty, vary your practice by volunteering at a free clinic, supervising interns through an agency, or taking trauma training to assist in disaster relief.

You should focus your working life in ways that combine your mission with what you love to do, are great at doing and that fulfill a variety of experiences.

— Marshall Goldsmith (2007)

Put thought to paper, teach a college course or weekend seminar, contribute an article to your local professional organization, develop a web site or blog.

Creativity has to do with really noticing the things that are without, and letting them bloom in the great within, and being available to the possibility of novelty.

— Jean Houston (1998)

❖ *Patience*

A martial arts student was studying a new set of movements under a master and asked how long it would take to learn the new skills. The master responded that it would take perhaps two years. Being a bit discouraged and impatient with this answer, the student asked how long it would take if he studied and worked very hard. To this the master responded, "in that case it would take about four years."

— Charles Manz (2002)

Have patience with everything unresolved, and try to love the questions themselves.

— Rainer Maria Rilke (1903)

The victim of domestic violence tells her story — it is a familiar one — and the apparent solution is obvious — to everyone but her. You want to persuade, to coax, to coerce, anything to get her to move on literally and figuratively. But you know that it won't be that way, that it will take weeks or months (if ever) to carefully lay the groundwork for her escape. When feeling impatient, you remind yourself of what your graduate supervisor said to you at your first meeting: 'If it was easy for your clients to change, they already would have done so.' Not only must we exhibit patience ourselves, we must also assist our clients to accept that gradual improvement is more likely than rapid transformation.

❖ A Case in Point

Regina had been sexually abused throughout her childhood — a minister, a grandfather, an uncle. Her mother, as is often the case in such matters, had not rushed to her defense and instead blamed the messenger. As an adult, Regina was nonresponsive sexually and came to therapy determined to overcome her problems. She was the perfect client: When asked to read a chapter of *The Courage to Heal* (Bass & Davis, 2002), she read the entire book; she kept a journal; she practiced assertion and self-care. However, after a month she felt frustrated at the pace of her progress and stated, "What else can I do to improve? I must get over these issues now, so I can be normal and get on with my life." In such cases, we must be careful not to absorb our client's impatience but instead help them accept that emotional healing, like its physical counterpart, has its own timetable that cannot be hurried.

❖ Putting It into Practice

Avoid the tendency to "speed up" therapy by filling in the silences with questions or comments. Therapy is not as portrayed in movie or television dramas in which pauses and silences are nearly nonexistent. In the real world clients need time to reflect on what has been said, to consider what they want to discuss next, and to recover emotionally from exploring difficult material.

My few early attempts to promote more rapid communication by filling in some of the pauses and hesitations in my clients' speech met with negative responses and continued pauses. Adaptation to the many silences required conscious effort on my part to stay attentive and focused during some of these very labored communications.

— Stephen Kahn and Erika Fromm (2000)

Perform a self-assessment to determine which types of clients tend to test your patience most. Many clinicians find it particularly difficult to deal with those clients who do not want to be in therapy in the first place. Reluctant spouses, rebellious children, and those who have been court ordered to therapy can often try the patience of even the most long-suffering therapists.

When therapy is compulsory, therapists can be defined as agents of the state. In such cases, therapists must redefine the situations as one in which they are on the side of the client...trying to help them avoid the situation from happening again.

— Jay Haley (1991)

Recognize that real and enduring changes require not just external behavioral changes but also corresponding changes in brain function. Such neurological modifications require significant time and patience on the parts of both client and therapist.

Building new brain networks that change emotional habits requires effort, determination, and practice. We must practice a great deal to learn a new emotional skill, and we must keep practicing to maintain that skill.

— David McMillan (2005)

❖ *Positive Expectations*

Make the expectations lively enough, and action will follow.

— Mason Cooley (1989)

The witch doctor, the physician, the therapist, believe that what they do will make a difference. They have faith in their powers to cure and to promote change.

— Jeffrey Kottler (2003)

Whether you think you can or think you can't — you are right.

— Henry Ford (date unknown)

Expectations have been found to have powerful effects in a variety of contexts (Rubie-Davies, 2007, de Jong & Peters, 2007). Teachers who expect more, get more; those who expect less, receive less. Hypnotists recognize that their expectations are as important as their inductions. The apparent expectations of researchers can sway experimental subjects. A positive correlation has been found between therapist expectations and therapy outcome (Curry, Rohde, Simons, Silva, Vitiello, & Kratochvil et al., 2006; Gaudiano & Miller, 2006).

Obviously, the more straightforward the client's problem, the easier it is to have positive outcome expectations. But what of the cases that are more complex, more troubling, more long-standing? What we tell ourselves about a case can enhance our belief in a positive outcome. We can focus on the half-empty glass or do what father of cognitive therapy, Aaron Beck (2001), would recommend and avoid the cognitive distortion of the "negative filter."

❖ A Case in Point

Gil was a male with gender identity problems, unmanageable anger leading to run-ins with the police, epileptic seizures, and as one might expect, a childhood from hell. When Dr. Flowers first accepted the case from referral, he saw the case as an interesting challenge. After the assessment though, he thought that he was way over his head — who wouldn't? During the first three years of treatment, there were many setbacks, hospitalizations, seizures in the office, and angry outbursts in which furniture was destroyed. At times the therapist despaired of ever really helping Gil, but at such times he would remind himself that the client deserved the best he could give of energy, enthusiasm, and expectations of growth. Somehow week by week, month by month, year by year, Gil made steady progress. Today Gil works very effectively at a home for the developmentally disabled, has resolved the gender problems having become a "she," and is an active mental health advocate. Now when Dr. Flowers gets discouraged with a case and begins to lose the ability to transmit positive expectations with a client, couple, or family, he thinks of Gil, with whom he still has contact about twice a year when she is in town and wants a mental health checkup.

❖ Putting It into Practice

Appreciate the fact that most clients come to therapy voluntarily, and although they may resist change, some part of them wants a better life.

Just as we encourage clients to believe in their ability to change, so must we exhibit a corresponding belief that they can expect to alleviate their distress with our support.

— Bruce Wampold (2001)

Focus on any sign of progress and celebrate it both personally and with the client.

The therapist maintains the clients' expectations of being helped by linking hope for improvement to the process of therapy.

— Rubin Battino (2006)

Note that it is nature's tendency to heal physical wounds and those wounds that deliberately eat away at our hearts and minds. Give yourself and the client time, space, safety, and a few tools to heal.

It is the physician's or healer's expectations for a cure, coupled with some active agent (pharmaceutical, physical, psychological), that permit the body and mind to heal.

— Jeffrey Kottler (2003)

❖ *Persistence*

Persistence is an underrated virtue in our profession. Some of therapy is just plodding. Looking at the eating journals of bulimic women, talking to a depressed student about exercise, or checking a mother on her use of time-outs — these things don't feel like making magic or yield impressive workshop videos.

— Mary Pipher (2003)

The man who removes a mountain begins by carrying away small stones.

— Chinese Proverb

Everyone falls down. You're not a failure until you don't get back up.

— Joey Green (2001)

Inventor Thomas A. Edison lost his laboratory in a fire that destroyed years of hard work worth millions of dollars — and he had no insurance. "What in the world will you do?" a reporter asked. "We will start rebuilding tomorrow morning," replied Edison (1914). Likewise, sometimes our clients' hard work in therapy does not seem to pay off, and we are faced with the question: "What do we do now?" Giving up on our clients is not an option for us, even though the world does not always support our best-drawn plans for success. Our therapeutic abilities are taxed as we help our clients rebuild, as did Edison and so many whose dreams do not initially materialize. So we convey our admiration for the attempts our clients make and keep our fingers crossed that enough attempts, enough lessons learned will eventually reap positive benefits.

❖ A Case in Point

One client struggled mightily to avoid his pattern of choosing "unavailable" men for romantic relationships. To alter this tendency and select well, he agreed to carefully assess his suitors' backgrounds: he introduced them to trusted friends for their impressions, asked in detail about the suitor's previous relationships, and was more gradual in moving toward physical intimacy. When he finally met a seemingly appropriate mate who cleared all the hurdles, he opened his carefully protected heart. As life would have it, his chosen one took a job overseas and he did not invite him along. His sense of hopelessness returned in duplicate, and the therapist had the daunting task of reinstilling both the client's and his own sense of hopefulness.

❖ Putting It into Practice

Recount the stories of individuals, both famous and unknown, who have persisted and resisted the temptation to throw in the towel. Michael J. Fox, Colin Powell, U2, Kelly Clarkson, and Benjamin Franklin all fell off the horse a time or two on the way to successful careers.

Elvis Presley's high school teacher in Memphis, Tennessee, gave him a C and told him he couldn't sing.

— Jerry Schilling and Chuck Crisafulli (2006)

When appropriate, use metaphors that highlight the increased probability of success with repeated attempts.

Most people don't realize that Babe Ruth, one of the great hitters of all time, struck out almost as many times as he hit a home run.

— Yogi Berra and David Kaplan (2001)

When clients experience failure, help them explore times in their lives when they have bounced back from disappointment. Often this requires patient and respectful questioning on the part of therapists to uncover forgotten experiences in which determination overcame the desire to quit.

80% of success is showing up.

— Woody Allen (1982)

❖ *Creativity*

Creativity makes a leap, then looks to see where it is.

— Mason Cooley (1996)

If science is its brain, creativity is the heart of therapy. It is the source of our intuition, the flexibility that leads to innovative models.

— Jeffrey Kottler (2003)

The creative act is fundamental to therapy if the therapist's goal is to identify patterns that are not working and assist clients in replacing these ineffective patterns with more efficacious ones.

— David Carson and Kent Becker (2003)

Early in a clinician's career, there is a tendency to utilize templates and standardized protocols to structure the path through assessment and treatment decisions. After a few years perhaps, the comfort zone expands and we begin to "think outside the box" or at least outside the manual. At such times, improvisation and creativity can occur, infusing energy into both the healer and the client. Unfortunately, the topic of therapeutic creativity is largely missing from clinical training programs. More and more the field resembles that of medicine and at its worst — automobile repair. We learn to diagnose, assess, and to implement predetermined manualized treatment plans. Could it be that much of what we call therapist burnout relates to the lack of room for the creative act in doing therapy?

❖ A Case in Point

Cloe Madanes, a family therapist in the tradition of Virginia Satir, recounts a case she supervised of a couple who could have been the quintessential guests on the Jerry Springer Show. Oliver had a temper and was proud to describe how he threw plates of food against the wall when upset. Caitlyn was an alcoholic and diabetic. They complained that their house was a total mess and that no one cared enough to do anything about it. They dressed carelessly. The therapist, an intern (who because of this couple was considering a career change), could not get them to follow through on any actions that would resolve their goal to "clean up their house."

Dr. Madanes recommended that the intern tell the couple that they reminded him of Scarlett and Rhett in Gone with the Wind, fighting all the time but having great passion for each other underneath it all. He then suggested that the intern ask them to recount their best memory together. They remembered early in their relationship a visit to a dolphin sanctuary. The intern then focused therapy on creating "new memories" that they would still recall ten years later. The therapist emphasized that neither of them would be able to recall who took out the trash ten years hence, but memories like the dolphin experience would be a pleasure forever. Each week they created one new positive memory, and this created the therapeutic momentum necessary to tackle their other marital and personal issues (Madanes, 1992).

❖ Putting It into Practice

Consider that creativity is an essential part of the therapeutic process.

Research on the nature of professional expertise makes it clear that highly skilled practitioners across a range of fields respond to relevant situations in a flexible, creative and contextually sensitive fashion.

— Donald Schon (2003)

Emphasize collaborative brainstorming whenever possible as a means of problem resolution. This process engages and empowers clients and allows the therapist to generate creative and client-specific solutions.

Creative thinking is tentative and exploratory. It is oriented to the development of possibilities rather than data, to speculation rather than to conclusions.

— Robert Leahy and E. Thomas Dowd (2003)

Recognize that creativity does not require enormous breakthroughs to be of value.

Thinking and producing creatively do not always involve a major restructuring of acquired knowledge or the creation of something entirely new, but often simply the reproductive application of past methods in useful and novel ways.

— John Dacey and Kathy Lennon (1998)

❖ *Credibility*

You'll be believed if you speak with authority.

— Anton Pavlovich Chekhov (1860-1904)

Credibility... is the constellation of characteristics that makes certain individuals appear worthy of belief, entitled to confidence, reliable and trustworthy.

— Derald Sue and Donald Sue (2003)

The mettle of professional credibility and competence... is dependent not upon the rule of expediency, success or technological triumph, but on the moral integrity of the therapeutic stance.

— Karl A. Menninger (1985)

It comes as a surprise to beginning therapists that their insights and recommendations are often met with skepticism instead of acceptance, resistance instead of respect. Why the skepticism? The issue is credibility. Social psychologist Stanley Milgram (1963) demonstrated the power of credibility in his famous experiments, which investigated to what lengths people would go "on the command of an authority." He asked subjects to shock people (confederates) when they made a mistake in a memory task. When the experimenter wore a white lab coat, the subjects were much more willing to inflict pain on the supposed victim. Therapists no longer wear white lab coats, so how can we enhance our credibility?

David Johnson's (1991) research indicates that several helper characteristics are involved in gaining client respect. First, we need to demonstrate expertise, not only by displaying diplomas, awards, and licenses but also by alluding to relevant experiences with the client's presenting problems. Reliability is also a significant factor: clients must know that they can depend on us, that we are consistent and predictable. Finally, we must come across as dynamic and confident that what we say and recommend can make a difference.

❖ A Case in Point

Victoria, a thirty-three-year-old former student of Dr. Flowers, had passed the national written exam on the first try but had failed the state oral exam a grand total of seven times. Somewhat embarrassed, she asked for a consultation with her former mentor. She told Dr. Flowers that the feedback from the examiners was that she was "not ready for unsupervised independent practice." To assess the problem, which was certainly not her clinical skills, Dr. Flowers asked her to come to their next session dressed as if she were taking the oral exam. As the mock oral exam proceeded, it became apparent that not only was her attire too provocative for such an occasion but also, due to nervousness, she was answering questions in a high-pitched voice that lacked authoritativeness. By the following oral exam, she had learned to slow down her responses, lower her pitch, and dress more formally for the occasion. Her increased "credibility" allowed her to pass the exam on her eighth try — with flying colors (just in time for the Board of Psychology to no longer require this type of exam).

❖ Putting It into Practice

When encouraging clients to explore new ways of thinking or behaving, always emphasize how that change will enhance the client's life, as opposed to how it will please the therapist.

The clearer it is to the client that it is his interests, and not the helper's, toward which the helper is working, the greater the credibility.

— Arnold Goldstein (1966)

Utilize appropriate assessment instruments as a means, not only to gather useful information about the client but also to promote the belief in therapist credibility and expertise as well.

Assessment tools which are used early in therapy... and occasionally during the course of treatment, can aid in treatment effectiveness, client morale and the perception that the therapist has expertise about the clinical problem.

— Curtis Booraem et al. (1992)

Before recommending a course of action, carefully question the client to determine which strategies she or he has already employed.

When therapists don't listen to their client's descriptions of what they have already tried, they run the risk of recommending a remedy that has failed previously. The therapist's credibility is thereby diminished.

— John Sommers-Flannagan and
Rita Sommers-Flannagan (2002)

The Therapist Acts

When in doubt, don't.

— Sigmund Freud (1995)

E arly in therapy, we focus on building a strong therapeutic relationship, which we infuse with caring, optimism, and patience. By doing so, we are poised to engage in the nuts and bolts of clinical work, the therapeutic strategies that can lead to healing, personal growth, and conflict resolution. The task then becomes to help clients focus on the most salient aspects of their struggles, to join with them in creating healthier coping skills, and to gently remind them when they veer too far from the path to positive personal change. Sometimes, as Freud observes in the quotation above, it is best to err on the side of caution when taking action with clients — to rely on interventions and procedures that have stood the test of time and those that the client is likely to be receptive to.

❖ Problem Solving

Sometimes people ask if it is depressing to spend all day listening to problems. I tell them, "I am not listening to problems, I am listening for solutions."

— Mary Pipher (2003)

It is commonplace that a problem stated is well on its way to solution ...

— John Dewey (1998)

Our daily lives are replete with situational problems which we must solve in order to maintain an adequate level of effective functioning.
                                                — Marvin Goldfried et al. (2000)

We can apply Freud's famous maxim "Sometimes a cigar is just a cigar" to how we approach assessing and treating our client's concerns. That is, sometimes a client's problem is just a problem that can profit from systematic problem solving. This process is the opposite of "winging it" or acting impulsively, an approach the typical client uses all too frequently. It involves helping clients delineate a problem, describe obstacles, generate alternative strategies and tactics, and then determine which are most likely to resolve the issues — certainly not the most colorful of therapeutic interventions, but perhaps one of the most useful. Problem-solving strategies have been used effectively in crisis situations and other major life upheavals, such as divorce and entering college, with substance abusers following residential treatment and children of all ages dealing with interpersonal conflict. Perhaps the best thing about learning problem-solving skills is that once learned they can be generalized to an infinite array of situations.

❖ A Case in Point

Marabella, a twenty-year-old Latina, was anxious and depressed because she was failing in school in spite of her above average IQ. A family doctor prescribed antidepressant medication and referred her to a cognitive behavioral therapist. The therapist had her challenge her negative thinking that because she was failing in school she was a failure as a person. She encouraged her to engage more frequently in pleasant activities. After several months of feeling no better and doing no better in school, Marabella visited the college psychological services. The counselor was familiar with the pressures placed on many young Latinas to value their family responsibilities before educational or career goals. In Marabella's case, her grandmother's continual requests for assistance and attention interrupted her studying at home. Marabella and her therapist brainstormed some ways to deal with this situation, and she chose the solution of studying more frequently at the college library. By the end of the semester, she had attained a B average and her depression had abated.

❖ Putting It into Practice

Initiate therapy with an emphasis on delineating the client's salient problems and educating the client about problem-solving procedures.

If therapy is to end properly, it must begin properly — by negotiating a solvable problem and discovering the social situations that make the problem necessary.

— Jay Haley (1991)

Help clients to accept some responsibility for their problems.

We can only hope to resolve problems whose existence we attribute (at least in part) to ourselves.

— Jeffrey Bedell (1997)

Take the lead when generating alternative strategies, but encourage, coax, and, if appropriate, build on the suggestions contributed by the client.

Sometimes effective alternatives can be generated when "wild ideas" are welcomed by the therapist. These ideas frequently can be modified into good solutions.

— Robert Sherman (1991)

Encourage clients to develop solutions by having them think of someone they know who is an effective problem solver and consider what actions such a person might take with the problem at hand.

The object is to see the problem from a fresh vantage point. The client tries to imagine how this other person would act by asking the question: "If so and so were in my shoes what would he or she do?"

— Morgan Jones (1998)

❖ *Collaborating*

Owing to an egg's shape, a beast banging on it from the outside will have great trouble breaking it open. But the slightest tap from the inside of the shell can shatter it. . . . By the same token, a

patient…tapping even lightly can accomplish more personality change than even the best therapist working alone from the outside.
— George Weinberg (2000)

Collaboration empowers clients by giving them a say in their own therapeutic process — and it fosters self-efficacy.
— Colin Feltham and Ian Horton (2000)

How can the therapist change the relationship to one of equality when every act of help, guidance or giving a directive defines the relationship as unequal and the client as being helped by a helper?
— Jay Haley (1991)

At one end of the spectrum of leadership styles is the "dictator"; at the other end is the lack of leadership where "anarchy" reigns. Where along this continuum should therapists position themselves? Certainly, there has been an evolution of thinking in this regard. Early on in the development of psychotherapy, clinical work was totalitarian in nature; that is the therapist was totally in charge: "You will lie down; you will free associate; you will accept my interpretation; you will attend therapy until I decide you should terminate." Healing was viewed from a medical model, with the identified healer acting upon the identified client. Gradually this perspective has evolved to a recognition that mental health clinicians are merely catalysts for change. As the spiritual teacher Ram Dass (1971) has put it, "All acts of healing are ultimately our selves, healing our Self." Thus, we do not directly heal our clients; rather our job is to energize them to take an active role in their own healing. To do so means engaging more often in discussions instead of lectures; brainstorming instead of providing "the" solution; and eliciting client feedback, beginning in the first session and continuing until termination is mutually agreed upon.

❖ A Case in Point

Dr. Norville knew she had her hands full with her new client. Max, aged fifty-seven, was the prototypical resistant client. He clearly did not want to be in therapy, but his employer had made it a condition of retaining his job. He was a hard and dedicated worker, but he resented it when management made directives and on a number of occasions had heated arguments with fellow employees. We have all seen such cases — stone-faced, arms folded, checking his watch every five minutes. He was clearly at the "precontemplation" stage described by Norcross (2002): other people, not him, were the problem. Collaboration became the hallmark of the Dr. Norville's approach with Max. At every step of the therapeutic process, she invited Max's input. She asked if it would be all right to ask a few questions and if he would mind if she took notes. She stated that although the employer had some clear goals for Max, she was more interested in what his goals might be. At the beginning of each session, she asked Max what he would like to focus on. When developing specific treatment interventions and out of session activities, she always developed a list of options, with Max making the final determination of what actions would be undertaken. Consensus building helped establish a firm therapist-client alliance that then allowed the client to face up to the need to develop some more effective interpersonal skills.

❖ Putting It into Practice

Avoid statements that imply you are the primary source of wisdom and healing.

Starting the first session with a question such as "How can I help you?" can set the stage for a paternalistic relationship rather than a collaboration.

— Suzanne Bender and Edward Messner (2003)

Remember that we as therapists have expertise about certain types of problems, but clients have the greater expertise about themselves.

Psychotherapy is not effective because the clinician administers a healing elixir to a passive patient. Instead the power of the treatment lies in the collaboration between therapist and patient, with the patient acting as expert on the subject at hand, herself.

— David Carson and Kent Becker (2003)

Encourage collaboration by helping clients express their ideas about how they may best make changes. Bertolino and

Schultheis, in their book, *The Therapist's Notebook for Families*, suggest the following exercise to elicit such information:

Which one or more of the following statements is true of how you like to learn?

* ❖ By having something told to me over and over.
* ❖ By reading as much as I can on a subject.
* ❖ From the experiences of other people.
* ❖ By realizing rewards when I succeed.
* ❖ By making mistakes and learning from them.
* ❖ By being shown where I am wrong.

❖ *Engendering Hope*

Contrary to Alexander Pope's famous assurance, hope does not spring eternal in the human breast. Rather, it must be vigilantly nurtured through an active faith in the possibilities and preciousness of human life in process.

— Jerome Frank (1973)

Optimism doesn't wait on facts. It deals with prospects. Pessimism is a waste of time.

— Norman Cousins (1989)

We must accept finite disappointment, but we must never lose infinite hope.

— Martin Luther King, Jr. (1964)

Like the coach who rallies her players when they are outmatched and outscored and the steadfast teacher who helps a discouraged student tackle a tough math problem, we, as therapists, must first and foremost convey the message that the client's problems are resolvable, that there is "probable cause" for hope. We do this when we remind clients how they have overcome similar problems in the past, when we help them set goals, and when we show delight at their slightest progress toward those goals. In addition, therapists can help clients develop a positive "future vision" of themselves, one in which they have developed the skills and tenacity to overcome their struggles.

❖ A Case in Point

Gillian had been a heavy smoker for twenty years, and her health, stamina, and pocketbook all suffered from it. She agreed to write a letter to her therapist from six months in the future when she had freed herself from this habit. In the letter, she described how she was able to afford a summer vacation with the money she had saved, visiting her grandchildren and hiking with them in the mountains. She talked about going to the gym where she met new friends, who have expanded her interests and involvements in life. As Gillian imagined these new life possibilities, she began to attack her problem habit with greater vigor and determination than previously — using medication and a support group as adjuncts to her therapy.

Similarly, you can ask clients to imagine having a conversation in the future with a valued friend in which they discuss how they have changed and become more fulfilled. Projecting oneself into the future is the means by which we activate hopefulness, transforming it from a noun to a verb.

❖ Putting It into Practice

Recognize that regardless of the specific problem or therapeutic goal, a client's fundamental concern is whether there is reason to believe that things can improve.

The cruelest loss of all is the loss of hope.

— Judith Rabinor (2002)

Incorporate the concepts of "positive psychology" (as found in the work of clinicians such as Martin Seligman, Gerald Monk, and Michael Mahoney) in which you emphasize client strengths and resources instead of focusing on deficits.

Narrative therapy requires an optimistic orientation in which the (client) comes to view himself as a courageous victor, rather than the pathologized victim.

— Gerald Monk et al. (1996)

When working with clients whose problems seem beyond repair, remind yourself of the overwhelming evidence of human

resilience and creativity. The psychologist-director of a residential facility for delinquent boys describes one such case:

> *To see the gradual metamorphosis of a bitter, self-hating, and gratuitously delinquent teenager into a dynamic, intellectually, emotionally sophisticated, high achieving young man was to witness an amazing journey from despair to hope, from self-vilification to mature self-affirmation.*
>
> — Brian Thorne (2002)

❖ *Goal Setting*

> *The mind that has no fixed goal loses itself; for, as they say, to be everywhere is to be nowhere.*
>
> — Michel de Montaigne (1995)

> *Research found reductions in depressive symptoms six months after the inception of treatment when patients experienced goals consensus following the second session.*
>
> — Maarten Dormaar et al. (1989)

> *The act of goal setting may be the fundamental mechanism of change. Specifically, the goal-setting process may facilitate change by encouraging the individuals to clarify their expectations...and address their chosen goal.*
>
> — Amy Nitza (2005)

When we help clients set goals, we provide a road map for the process of therapy. When clients have a reasonably clear sense of the direction in which they are headed, there is an increased sense of motivation and purposefulness that innervates clinical work. It is no wonder that several studies have shown that goal setting early in treatment is directly related to positive therapeutic outcomes and that clients rate even individual sessions as more productive when specific goals have been addressed (Dormaar et al, 1989).

❖ A Case in Point

"Dazed and confused" were the words Kenny used to describe his life. He was not connected to anyone or anything. In college he coasted, doing the minimum. At home he fought with everyone. "Too shy" to ask girls out, he was extremely lonely. On paper, it looked like there would be plenty of goals to choose from. However, efforts to set goals were leaving the therapist dazed and confused. Finally at the end of a session, Kenny stated, "I have come up with a goal...it is to have a goal."

❖ Putting It into Practice

Through questioning, help clients move from general complaints about their lives to specific measurable outcomes that help to narrow the focus.

When president-elect Bill Clinton made his first visit to Washington after the 1992 presidential election, he took a walk through an economically depressed area nearby. One woman began telling him the woes of the city. In response, Clinton asked, "What do you want to change?" The woman looked a little startled and then, recovering, said something like this: "We want jobs. We want safe streets. We want the drug pushers out of our neighborhood."

— Gerald Egan (1994)

Providing a clear structure to the goal-setting process can enhance therapeutic outcomes.

Although it seems formal, I have found it useful to help clients create a written document which describes the goal, its rationale and the steps necessary for goal completion.

— Judith Beck (1995)

After formulating a general goal, delineate specific outcomes (subgoals) that can be accepted as minimum signs of improvement.

Setting a minimum goal for outcome supports the therapist's tactical aim of introducing a small but strategic change which can then initiate a ripple or domino effect leading to further positive developments.

— Alan Gurman and Neil Jacobson (2002)

❖ Confrontation

Confrontation in counseling is encouraged when therapists detect discrepancies between what clients are saying and what they have (previously) said; between what they are saying verbally and nonverbally and between the client's view of the problem and the way the therapist sees it.

— Susan Walen et al. (1992)

Now this is where I feel like I need to give you a kick in the butt. This is about you taking care of yourself, and what you're telling me is you don't take care of yourself. So I want to give you a kick in the butt.

— Lee Kassen (1996)

Confrontation plus caring brings growth. . . . These are two arms of a genuine relationship: confrontation with truth; affirmation with love.

— David Ausberger (1980)

One of the more pleasurable aspects of our job is to compliment clients when they have engaged in new and productive behaviors, when they have made positive changes. A less pleasant but equally necessary duty is to remind clients when they are off track, engaging in repeated self-defeating, unproductive, and destructive patterns of behavior or thought. These are moments where we must confront but not offend, inform but not insult. At such times, we are challenged to communicate with honesty, humility, and deep caring. Who among us hasn't profited at one time or another from a gentle but firm nudging from a family member, friend, teacher, or coach? Clinicians are also in a position to provide the needed push that can propel their clients to reach beyond their comfort zone toward a healthier, more fulfilling future.

❖ A Case in Point

Mel has assessed and reassessed the viability of his marriage and can find only reasons to end it — including the fact that his wife has been involved in serial affairs throughout the course of the marriage. He won't leave her, and she is seemingly content to have the best of both worlds, with the security of Mel and the excitement of the next romance. After a year of flip-flopping (mostly flopping), Mel once again tells the therapist he wishes he had the strength to move on. The therapist has reached his limit and decides that a firm confrontation is in order. He begins supportively and builds to an assertive crescendo: "I know how much you value the sanctity of marriage, but continuing in this relationship is taking a toll on your health and that of your wife as well. It seems that you fold whenever you try to tell your wife the marriage is over in person. You must start this process at a distance and stop worrying about doing this in the 'perfect' way with the 'perfect' words at the 'perfect' time. There is no way to deliver a message you both wish were not necessary without hurt." Though Mel is not thrilled with the messenger or the message, by the next session he has emailed his wife, and she has replied with "it's about time."

❖ Putting It into Practice

When confronting a client, diplomacy, tact, and sensitivity are of the essence. Nobody likes to hear that he has messed up yet again, and this is particularly true of clients who have difficulty taking directions or criticism from authority figures. Thus, it is useful to develop a repertoire of carefully worded statements that firmly but respectfully challenge the client, such as the following suggested by Beck et al. (2001):

- ❖ I don't get the feeling you're being completely straight with me right now.
- ❖ Are you being honest with yourself about this?
- ❖ I am a little confused because I have to admit that what you are saying doesn't fit with what you have told me before.
- ❖ I get the feeling you are struggling to tell me something.
- ❖ Take your time; I will listen to whatever news you have for me.

Document your clients' statements so that you can use their own words when confronting them instead of "sermonizing." Often the health-seeking part of your clients will tell you what they need to do or avoid doing, and when you remind them of these statements it softens the confrontation. For example, a substance-abusing client wished to discontinue therapy prematurely, so the therapist remarked:

I'm a little confused right now, you're telling me that everything's cool and that you can leave therapy, but I remember you told me that it would be times just like now that you are prone to relapsing... when you think everything is going great and you let your guard down — what do you think?

— Ellen Quick (1996)

Recognize that the risk of honest and humane confrontation is balanced by the possibility of substantial therapeutic progress.

A mixture of accurate empathy and skilled confrontation may actually strengthen the therapeutic relationship as well as help the client to overcome therapeutic roadblocks.

— Cory Newman et al. (2001)

❖ *Flexibility*

Whatever is flexible and flowing will tend to grow. Whatever is rigid and blocked will wither and die.

— Lao Tzu (Tao Te Ching)

All people filter incoming information... contradictory information is either ignored or quickly forgotten. Recognizing this, the conscientious scientist Charles Darwin made a special effort to write down instances that did not fit his hypotheses.

— Jerome Frank (1973)

And like a successful parent, the therapist needs flexibility. The ability to switch from one approach to another... to see the patient's life as a journey, to appreciate both the shoals and the magic of it, its specialness.

— Ilana Rabinowitz (1998)

It is natural at some point in a clinician's career to identify as a member of a particular theoretical school. Therapists, like all human beings, may find security in establishing allegiance to a system of theoretical beliefs. However, frequently therapists become too dogmatic, refusing to even entertain the possibility that their particular approach is not appropriate in all cases. Fortunately, the tunnel vision which often besets so many younger therapists gives way to a more open-minded approach. The authors of the book *Bad Therapy* (Kottler and Carlson, 2002) found this to be the case. In their interviews with twenty renowned clinicians, they found that theorists who were originally known for developing specific treatment methods were now "converging, borrowing ideas from one another, looking at commonalities in what they have discovered." It is this kind of flexibility that best serves our clients and keeps doing therapy a fresh enterprise.

❖ A Case in Point

Sigmund Freud's first recorded case involved a young woman (Elizabeth Von R.) who was unable to walk due to psychogenic disturbance. Freud claimed that her cure was the result of his use of the technique of "Abreaction." Irvin Yalom recounts, however, that a close examination of Freud's notes indicates that he used an "eclectic" approach to her treatment. He had her visit the grave of her sister and speak to a young man she was interested in (behavioral approaches). He intervened with her parents to encourage opening lines of communication (family systems work). He gave her financial advice, and dealt with her uncertainties about the future (cognitive restructuring). In other words, Freud was not a strict Freudian.

❖ Putting It into Practice

A clinician can incorporate specific techniques from various therapeutic schools without losing allegiance to a particular theoretical perspective. Using the "empty chair" technique does not make one a "Gestalt" therapist, and recognizing the need to connect with emotions does not mean you are a "Freudian."

One can be flexible enough to recognize the usefulness of interventions from a variety of sources without adopting "whole cloth" the entire theoretical orientation.

— Barbara Krasner and Austin Joyce (1995)

Avoid the dogmatic position of a "one-size-fits-all" approach to therapy. It is fine to have a solid theoretical base, but the human condition is much too complex to expect that all conditions will respond to one specific approach.

A large portion of success is derived from flexibility. It is all very well to have principles, rules of behavior concerning right and wrong. But it is quite as essential to know when to forget as when to use them.

— Alice Foote MacDougal (1928)

Retain the curiosity of the novice who is able to explore new perspectives with an open mind — without the bias of the expert.

I would walk twenty miles in my bare feet to see my worst enemy if I thought I could learn something from him.

— Carl Rogers (1961)

❖ ## Using Humor

Remarkably, when following up with clients after many years, they tended to remember a relevant joke I had told them and continued to draw comfort from a "wise narrative" I had related.

— Maurits Kwee (1990)

I made the joyous discovery that ten minutes of genuine belly laughter had an anesthetic effect and would give me at least two hours of pain-free sleep.

— Norman Cousins (1989)

I have seen what a laugh can do. It can transform almost unbearable tears into something bearable, even hopeful.

— Bob Hope (2004)

Chris Rock, George Lopez, Charlie Chaplin, Carol Burnett — all great comedians — and all had a childhood background of near intolerable hardship. Somehow they managed to turn their misery into mirth, their tears into laughter. It is a well-know fact that Abraham Lincoln endured great hardship in his life and often suffered from periods of deep depression. Less well known is the fact that he often surprised his associates with his ability to laugh even at the bleakest moments. Of course doing therapy is not an occasion for stand-up comedy, but a light touch at the right moment can be a healing agent, as potent as any therapeutic tool.

Research on the use of humor (Strean, 1993) indicates that it has the potential to produce positive effects in the cardiopulmonary and musculoskeletal systems of the body — quite a mouthful isn't it? It can reduce anxiety, increase morale, and allow for a broader perspective of the presenting problem. Lastly, sharing a laugh together can also enhance the therapist-client bond.

❖ A Case in Point

A man asked for an emergency appointment, and said in a urgent tone that he wanted some help because he was a latent homosexual . . . because over the last few months he was seeing images of naked men when he was having sex with his wife. I told him that I wasn't sure this made him a latent homosexual and that . . . human beings have a lot of strange things floating around in their minds — some meaningful, some not. I asked him what he would think if, while having sex with his wife, he had images of fire trucks — would this make him a latent fireman? He laughed and said he guessed not.

— Shelley Green and Douglas Flemons (2004)

❖ Putting It into Practice

The ways you can use humor are many and varied.

One therapist utilized a blowup doll of Godzilla to represent the client's "monster father"; Salvador Minuchin had a female client use a pen as a "magic wand" with which she could change herself in any way she saw fit. Sometimes we can use humorous anecdotes from our own lives that bear on the matter at hand. For example, when discussing a client's dysfunctional family, a therapist told his client, "Yes, that reminds me of my father's frequent admonition to me, 'always remember that your brother is an only child.'"

— Gene Combs and Jill Freedman (1990)

Remember that the best therapeutic humor is instructional as well as entertaining. As in the case of the latent firefighter described above, the humor is in the service of making a crucial therapeutic point — in this case, that thoughts and images are not necessarily indicative of emotional conflict.

Using humor in therapy is not only a fun way of learning, but also a potent teaching tool — as it allows us to express a message we might not wish to communicate directly.

    — George W. Burns [not the late comedian!!] (2001)

Avoid negative humor, that is, humor that pokes fun at individuals or that teases the client. One of the authors (Bernard Schwartz) had the following experience: a client at a college counseling center divulged to her therapist that she shared some of the questions on her final exam with a student who had the same class at a different time. The therapist lifted the phone, pretending to call the dean of students to inform him of the student's transgression — the student began to cry. The therapist felt like crying.

The Healer's Journey

*To become an expert, one does not have to be gifted or talented
or possess some sort of inherent intellectual inclination
toward superior performance. The evidence suggests that the
ordinary person can achieve expertise. However, the ordinary
person must invest extraordinary amounts of time, practice,
and commitment to develop expertise.*

— Len Jennings (2005)

*Expertness entails reaching a stage of "accumulated wisdom."
At this point "automacity" develops. This is akin to the expert
baseball player who no longer attends to specific batting
mechanics and thus is free to notice subtleties in the pace and
direction of the ball. For the therapist, this means being freed
from the mechanics of doing therapy and thus focusing on
subtle elements of the client's concerns and behavior.*

— Thomas Skovholt (2001)

It has been approximated that for chess players to reach the "masters" level it takes approximately ten to twenty thousand hours of focused practice. (This is equivalent to a college student putting in forty hours of study per week for ten years or so.) How many hours are necessary for therapists to become experts at their craft? In a study of over four thousand therapists in seven countries, Orlinsky, Ronnestad, and Botermans found that the "most salient positive influence on career development was direct clinical experience in therapy with clients" (2001). Of course practice alone will not create expertise. Commitment to professional and personal development, the willingness to seek guidance when appropriate, and personal characteristics such as patience, persistence, and passion all contribute to a clinician's progress from novice to master therapist.

❖ *Success*

It is natural, especially for new counselors, to measure success through client positive change and appreciation and by the reaction of supervisors and peers. The major problem is that the reactions of these individuals are outside the control of the counselor and lack of control is a major factor in occupational stress.

— Thomas Skovholt (2001)

Success… is peace of mind which is a direct result of self-satisfaction in knowing you made the effort to become the best that you are capable of becoming.

— John Wooden (2005)

The best augury of a man's success in his profession is that he thinks it the finest in the world.

— George Eliot (1876)

Doing therapy is a field in which "delayed gratification" is often the name of the game. The clinical endeavor is at the far end of the continuum from athletic pursuits in which minute by minute you know where you stand. Think about baseball. You throw a pitch — and instantly receive feedback in the form of a called strike or ball. You shoot a basket — it is a swish or a brick. Not so in our work. On occasion, we therapists may receive timely and positive feedback from our clients, but more often than not reinforcement is intermittent at best, nonexistent at worst. Thus, if we are waiting for accolades from the world, we shouldn't hold our breath. As Coach Wooden points out, while waiting for the external reinforcement we all appreciate it is best to focus on what we can do to better ourselves as people and as clinicians.

❖ A Case in Point

The authors had met for a brainstorming session at a local restaurant. Following the meal (getting less brainstorming done than planned), a woman rushed up, proclaiming excitedly, "You are Dr. Schwartz, right?" "Yes," I responded. "I want you to know that about seventeen years ago I brought my eight-year-old son to you for therapy because he was experiencing extreme anxiety every time his father traveled by plane on business trips. He is with me today and he said he never got the chance to thank you for helping him." In a flash the eight-year-old I remembered stood next to me — a grown man — and nearly toppled me with a warm bear hug while thanking me profusely for helping him overcome his phobia. Talk about delayed positive feedback!

❖ Putting It into Practice

Use client satisfaction surveys and short assessment tools. Brief scales such as the Working Alliance Inventory (Greenberg and Horvath, 1989) can provide direct positive feedback (and useful negative feedback as well) on the progress of therapy and the quality of the client-therapist relationship. The WAI contains twelve questions, which are rated on a five-point scale. Sample questions include:

❖ I am confident in my therapist's ability to help me.
❖ I believe the way we are working with my problem is correct.
❖ My therapist and I trust one another.
❖ I feel that my therapist appreciates me.

Each day, take time to review the positive experiences that have occurred in your clinical work. The human mind is more geared toward remembering negatives — what went wrong, and what could go wrong — than those things that went well or were accomplished. This negative bias can wear down those in the helping professions if not balanced with remembering accomplishments as well as failures.

One effective assignment we give depressed patients is to have them simply replay at the end of the day three things that went well that day. This simple act is often a catalyst for a lifting of mood and attitude.

— Martin Seligman (2006)

❖ Dealing with Failure and Criticism

Failure is the foundation of success and the means by which it is achieved.

— Lao Tzu (*Tao Te Ching*)

One of the major ways of learning is through mistakes. They provide clues for further growth.

— Arnold Lazarus

When Thomas Edison's experiments with a storage battery failed to produce any positive results, the inventor refused to concede defeat: "I've just found ten thousand ways that won't work."

— Joey Green (2001)

There are many ways to look at therapeutic failure, some of which are more beneficial to our psyches than others. In his writing about resilience, Martin Seligman (2006) identified three personality characteristics of those who do not bounce back from personal failure: personalization, persistence, and pervasiveness.

❖ When we **personalize** our mistakes, we blame ourselves totally for the situation. For example, if a client states that she is not happy with the direction of therapy, you question your clinical judgment or skills. A more beneficial approach is to accept your fallibility but to also consider external factors, such as that the client is not responding to the standard treatment plan, and thus the direction or clinical approach needs to be reevaluated and adjusted.

❖ Worse than personalization is the tendency to view a poor result as evidence of future and **persistent** failure. On the other, healthier hand, the resilient individual views the incident as a "sample of one" and rather than engaging in detrimental fortune-telling simply goes back to the drawing board, assuming a more optimistic outcome the next time.

❖ **Pervasiveness** is the tendency to conclude that a setback in one area of life is evidence of being a failure in general. For example, one therapist found that he was not being effective in working with eating-disordered clients. He concluded if he couldn't help this particular client group that he was a total failure as a clinician. A healthier view is one that accepts the reality that not everyone is a generalist and that difficulty in one clinical realm does not necessarily reflect a pervasive lack of clinical skills.

Of course, lack of success with a client is never going to feel good. A certain amount of reflection and concern is natural. However, the quality of the reflection and the avoidance of Seligman's "three Ps" (2006) can greatly influence whether we carry on, burdened by the past, or with confidence and optimism.

❖ A Case in Point

Larissa was an extremely shy college student whose few friends had scattered after high school to prestigious universities while she was struggling to pass her courses in a community college. She felt inferior academically and socially, living an isolated life devoid of outside interests except for volleyball, which she had played in high school. After months of clinical work, she had finally joined an adult volleyball league, found a job (her first), sought out tutoring, and began to interact more with students and faculty. In spite of all this behavioral change and concurrent cognitive work, her depression worsened and her therapist referred her to another psychologist while maintaining intermittent contact for continuity. The therapist was so distressed by this apparent "failure" that she entered therapy herself. She thought that she should suspend her practice because she felt totally responsible for the outcome in this case. Her personalization and a fear of persistent failure in the future had overtaken her in spite of her years of success in developing a successful and effective practice.

❖ Putting It into Practice

As clinicians, we need to expect disappointment from time to time. To believe that we can help every client with every kind of problem is to create highly unrealistic expectations regarding our abilities and ignores the limits of our profession.

God doesn't require us to succeed; he only requires that you try.

— Mother Teresa (1992)

Although we cannot succeed in every case, we can reduce client dropout or poor therapeutic outcome by carefully assessing and responding to the client's level of commitment to change. Often therapists initiate behavioral change interventions prematurely — before the client has decided that change is necessary. In such cases, therapeutic failure increases dramatically.

Only 20 percent of patients seeking therapy for a variety of problems including substance abuse, obesity and health concerns are at the "action stage." The majority are at the precontemplation or contemplation stage.

— John Norcross et al. (1994)

When therapeutic progress is stymied, consider consultation with a colleague to gain a fresh perspective. Frequently therapists with difficult cases prematurely make a referral to another psychologist or stubbornly continue utilizing the same conceptual framework.

To admit we are stuck garners the respect of fellow clinicians. In fact, I often make referrals to therapists who have consulted with me in the past because I trust them to do their best for their clients.

— John Karter (2002)

❖ *Self-Care*

Another time after a long day of work, I came home with a migraine. My son repeatedly tried to talk to me, and I kept impatiently signaling that I needed my space. Finally, he handed me his allowance and asked, "If I pay you would you talk to me?"

— Mary Pipher (2003)

Although each of us experience distress differently, the literature points to moderate depression, mild anxiety, emotional exhaustion, and disrupted relationships as the common residue of immersing ourselves in the inner worlds of distressed and distressing people.

— Joan Brady et al. (1995)

I have always been better at caring and looking after others than caring for myself. But in these later years, I have made progress.

— Carl Rogers (1961)

At the beginning of this book, we described the many challenges facing clinicians as they try to enhance the lives of their clients. But what about the therapist's life? Certainly, feeling competent is a major component of our sense of well-being. However, there are other challenges that we face in life besides professional success. These challenges include meeting our social and recreational needs, avoiding burnout, and participation in professional development. We never want to reach that place in our career when we reply to the question "How was your day?" with the too often heard "Same old, same old." One dire consequence of lack of self-care is therapist burnout. Christina Maslach (2003) described burnout as a syndrome that can lead to feelings of low personal accomplishment, emotional exhaustion, and depersonalization — a state in which the therapist develops negative, cynical attitudes toward clients and clinical work. Therapists who develop burnout are at great risk for leaving the field. Thus, lack of self-care can affect every aspect of a therapist's personal and professional life.

❖ A Case in Point

Clara, aged forty-five, had built a successful clinical practice over a number of years but was brought before the Board of Psychology amidst "abandonment" allegations brought by a former client. It seems she had a client with borderline and narcissistic features who exerted borderline-like pressure to engage in social contact with Clara beyond the therapy hour. She wanted desperately for Clara to attend her daughter's wedding, an award ceremony at work, her son's school play. The play was Clara's undoing. She inadvertently insulted the client by jokingly stating that her son's performance was a "bit over the top." The client went from idolizing to villainizing Clara, suing her in civil court and of course reporting her to the appropriate board. The board appointed a "monitor," an experienced therapist, who helped Clara understand her own vulnerability to engaging in boundary-crossing behavior. First of all Clara was recently divorced, which led to financial pressures, which led to seeing too many clients, which led to a lack of social life and support. The monitor stepped in and strongly encouraged Clara to reduce her client load, take regular vacations, preferably with friends, and develop new interests such as yoga. In common terms, she was helped to "get a life."

❖ Putting It into Practice

Be vigilant for warning signs of therapist overload such as increased irritability with clients, decreased interest in reading journals or attending conferences, and increased procrastination in completing reports or calling back clients.

> *The lives of others, their hopes, ideas, goals, aspirations, pains, fears, despair, anger — are in focus... out of the illuminated microscope we lose sight of our own needs.*
>
> — Carl Rogers (1961)

Avoid overspecialization in which you exclusively see clients with one clinical disorder. Today there are more and more specialty areas — eating disorders, domestic violence, child-custody, abuse, and sexual dysfunction to name a few. To keep it fresh, try to include at least a few cases from other clinical domains, and engage in other options for professional involvement — mentoring, research, and organizational work.

> *On the one hand developing a specialization can help build a practice by creating a therapeutic niche — on the other hand, the lack of novelty can lead to burnout.*
>
> — Christina Maslach (2003)

A balanced work life is not enough. The best therapists are those who live rich lives outside of their clinical world: family, travel, ongoing educational experiences, recreational and spiritual development. Not only do these experiences enrich our lives, they broaden our perspectives and re-energize our work.

> *Live a balanced life, learn some and think some*
> *and draw and paint and sing and dance*
> *and play and work every day some.*
>
> — Robert Fulghum (1989)

Healing the Deeper Wounds

Healing inner wounds involves repairing the self that has been split asunder. It is a process of making connections, of listening to symptoms, and hearing what it is they have to say. And even though psychotherapists can't mend torn psyches with needle and thread, we can help people recover themselves.

— Leslie Shore (1995)

Even the most pervasive wounds can be a bridge to potential personal transformation.

— E. Mark Stern (1991)

And then there are the clients who come to us with psychic pain of a greater magnitude than most. They have suffered life-shattering wounds, losses, and trauma that have permeated their core, causing disruptions in their development, their relationships, and their faith in the goodness of humanity or themselves. In many of these cases time alone has not healed, and, in fact, the unresolved pain has become increasingly burdensome as the years have progressed. Healing these deeper wounds means that the client must face that which they never would have wished to face in the first place. It means confronting a depth of feeling that has proven overwhelming. Accompanying our clients on this healing journey requires our greatest patience as well as our appreciation of the gradual nature of the healing process.

❖ *Grieving and Loss*

My own relationship breakup has taught me to never underestimate the intensity of another's experience, but to listen closely and to learn from it.

— Susan Anderson (2000)

The bereaved must achieve some balance that allows them to experience their pain, sense of loss, loneliness, fear, anger, guilt and sadness; to let in their anguish and let out their expressions of anguish and yet to do all this in doses, so as to not be overwhelmed by these feelings.

— Gwen Schwartz-Borden (1986)

The mind has a dumb sense of vast loss.... It will take mind and memory months and possibly years to gather the details and thus learn and know the whole extent of the loss.

— Mark Twain (1871)

The loss of family members, friends, or romantic relationships often gives rise to the deepest of human wounds. Grievers speak of feeling "shattered" and often wonder how they will ever pick up the pieces of their lives and continue forward. Before we can assist our clients as they work through the grieving process, we must first and foremost provide appropriate empathy, support, and a safe space to express deep emotion. Unsurprisingly, those therapists who are the most empathic are those who have suffered similar losses. But what about the times when our clients' loss is totally foreign to our experience?

❖ A Case in Point

An intern recounted such an experience when she told her supervisor that a client of hers had strongly rebuked her for responding in a "cold and distant manner" when she had tearfully shared the pain of having to put her beloved dog to sleep. The intern explained that her parents never allowed her to have a pet as a child, thus she found it difficult to appreciate the depth of feeling one could have for animals. At such times, perhaps the best we can do is apologize profusely and expand our definition of what to consider significant personal loss.

In addition to empathy, clients dealing with significant loss require our enduring patience, for as the quotations by Mark Twain and Schwartz-Borden indicate, we come to cope with loss in "small doses" over "months and possibly years." However, mourning is not a passive phenomenon in which time alone heals all. Rather it's an active process involving surmounting several pivotal "tasks of mourning." J. William Worden in his book *Grief Counseling and Grief Therapy* (2001) describes three such tasks to which therapists must turn their attention to assist clients who have become stalled during the mourning process.

❖ Putting It into Practice

Help clients accept the reality of the loss. Those stuck at this stage may use "denial" to avoid acceptance of the loss. For example, Queen Victoria continued to lay out her deceased husband's clothing each day and often went around the palace speaking to him. Others use denial in the opposite way — not by denying the loss, but by denying that the loss has any significance — acting as if it is "no big deal" when in reality it is an all too painfully big deal.

At times mourners seem to be under the influence of reality and behave as if they fully accept that the deceased is gone. At other times they behave irrationally, under the sway of the fantasy of eventual reunion.

— George Krupp et al. (1986)

Help clients work through the pain of grief. The grief process cannot be rushed, but it can be hindered when mourners and their friends and well-wishers minimize the significance of the loss. Those who mean well often dispense platitudes: "You are young and can have another child." "Life is for the living and he wouldn't want you to feel this way." If we are not careful in our attempts to console, we can send a subtle message that our clients should not feel what they are feeling, that they do not need to grieve.

Because it is necessary for the bereaved person to go through the pain of grief in order to move forward, then anything that continually allows the person to avoid this pain can be expected to prolong the course of mourning.

— Colin Parkes (2001)

Help the client adjust to an environment and life circumstances that have changed after the loss. At this stage we help clients make external adjustments to the loss (how it affects everyday functioning), internal adjustments (one's self-definition, esteem, and efficacy), and spiritual adjustments (how the loss affects one's beliefs, values, and assumptions). Thus, we are ever patient and gentle as our clients move toward acceptance, celebration of what they experienced, and integration of the loss into a future orientation.

On how one achieves this task, turns the outcome of mourning — either progress toward a recognition of life's changed circumstances, or. . . a state of suspended growth in which one is held prisoner by a dilemma that cannot be solved.

— John Bowlby (1997)

❖ *Treating Trauma Victims*

The troubles of the young seem to be soon over; they leave no external mark. If you wound the tree in its youth the bark will quickly cover the gash; but when the tree is very old, peeling the bark off, and looking carefully, you will see the scar there still. All that is buried is not dead.

— Olive Schreiner (2003)

Resilience is not a trait that people either have or don't have. It involves behaviors, thoughts, and actions that can be learned and developed in anyone. A primary factor in resilience is having caring and supportive relationships that provide love and trust, that provide role models, and that offer encouragement and reassurance.

— Ximena Mejia (2005)

Continuous appreciation of the client's bravery is a central task for the clinician in trauma cases. . . this means taking note of the strength that is required to confront painful memories when avoidance is so obviously the less challenging option.

— J. William Worden (2001)

A traumatic experience is like no other in that it often takes on a life of its own, inserting itself into every aspect of the survivor's life with recollections, nightmares, and avoidances of related cues.

Physiologically it can elicit a perpetual state of vigilance, resulting in sleep pattern disturbance, irritability, angry outbursts, and difficulty concentrating. The experience of trauma can alter a person's entire worldview — causing survivors to question the trustworthiness of people, nature, governments, even God. All too often treatment for posttraumatic stress disorder has focused almost exclusively on helping the client desensitize to the traumatic event. In this regard therapists have employed various models, including traditional relaxation and visualization, eye movement desensitization and reprocessing, and hypnosis. However, trauma recovery requires comprehensive and multifaceted protocol that addresses the client's behavioral, cognitive, and perhaps spiritual domains.

Treatment also requires a process of "re-education." First, we must convey that the client's suffering was not of her or his own doing and that it should in no way be minimized. For example, many victims of domestic violence feel responsible for their spouse's aggression and may have "learned" that some male aggression is normal and to be expected within marriage. The next "learning objective" in trauma recovery involves the concept of resilience — the idea that human beings are capable of healing even from the direst of experiences. Lastly, we must try to rebuild our client's negative image of the world, replacing it with a more balanced and positive view of humankind, nature, and life. Trauma makes the world appear unsafe, unfair, and unpredictable. All of us "know" the world is not totally fair or safe, but the person who has experienced and internalized trauma knows this in a way that affects brain function, physiology, and very possibly neurochemistry. We can help "reteach" the trauma victim about the world through a number of interventions and assignments, as well as through our own expression of caring and compassion.

❖ A Case in Point

All losses are hurtful; some are traumatic. Elana had put off having children as have many successful professionals, but she started to hear the ticking of the biological clock and so in her mid-thirties she cut back on work, married, and made plans to start a family. However, within days of her marriage, her husband had a sudden brain aneurism and died. In spite of the trauma, Elana handled the loss as well as can be expected. After a period of grief and healing, she was able to carry on with life and five years later was able to fall in love and remarry. After months of trying to become pregnant, she attempted in vitro fertilization, which required months of bed rest after implantation. The process was successful and Elana gave birth to twins. However, due to severe respiratory problems both children died within the year, as is often the case with in vitro fertilization.

The compounded losses in her life resulted in the clear symptomatology of posttraumatic stress disorder including flashbacks and nightmares involving the removal of life supports for one of the children, numbing and depersonalization experiences, and panic attacks when confronted with cues that reminded her of hospitals or doctors. In addition to these symptoms, she started to question every aspect of her life: "Should she have tried to start a family at her age? Was she worthy of her husband's love? Where was she to find purpose and meaning in her life?"

Therapy in this case involved a rebuilding of faith in herself, her future, and her view of the world as a place that can provide meaning and pleasure. Elana had to start by looking for and being able to acknowledge that which even verged on pleasure. She had to battle guilt by tracking and challenging self-condemning thoughts. Elana was frozen about making any decisions whatsoever, and thus had to relearn making choices to reclaim confidence, starting with simple ones like what one thing she could do out of the house this week or what to order in a restaurant. Gradually the topic of family was introduced, and after a year and a half of therapy, she and her husband decided on adoption.

The recovery from trauma in Elana's case is still progressing — but along with the support of her husband and two adopted children, she has regained a sense of her ability to endure and engage with life once again.

❖ Putting It into Practice

Redefine the client's "reliving symptoms" (nightmares, flashbacks) as adaptive attempts at healing rather than as

pathological responses. Of course, you must immediately address symptom reduction and safety concerns. However, it is important for clients to recognize that their symptoms are attempts to internally resolve distressing thoughts, feelings, and memories. This understanding sets the stage for "therapeutic exposure" techniques, which can be seen as interventions that optimize those activities in which the client is already engaging.

> *Seen in this light, traumatized individuals are not collections of symptoms but rather people, who, at some level, are attempting to recover — albeit not always successfully.*
>
> — John Briere and Catherine Scott (2006)

Recognize and communicate to the sufferer of posttraumatic stress disorder that trauma not only causes great distress and adversity but can frequently result in significant personal growth as well. This may involve new levels of psychological resilience, additional survival skills, greater self-knowledge and self-appreciation, increased empathy, and a broader, more complex view of life in general.

> *The widow may learn new independence; the survivor of a heart attack may develop a more healthy perspective on life's priorities; and the person exposed to a catastrophic event may learn important things about his or her resilience.*
>
> — Anna Baranowsky et al. (2005)

Promote actions that minimize the client's sense of "victimization" and helplessness. Trauma victims can be empowered by engaging in behaviors in which they focus on meeting their own needs for safety and by contributing to the well-being of others. Such actions include the following:

> *Increasing the client's sense of personal safety by recommending living areas which are "neighbor-friendly." Utilizing pets, especially dogs, as both sources of comfort and safety. Emphasizing concern for others in need through volunteerism. Helping clients to establish daily routines and create plans for a fulfilling future.*
>
> — Matthew Friedman (2006)

❖ *The Paralysis of Shame*

*The difference between guilt and shame is very clear. . . . We feel
guilty for what we do. We feel shame for what we are. A person feels
guilt because he did something wrong. A person feels shame because
he is something wrong. We may feel guilty because we lied to our
mother. We may feel shame because we are not the person our mother
wanted us to be.*

— Lewis B. Smedes (1996)

*Moderately painful feelings about specific behaviors motivate people
to behave in a moral, caring manner. . . . But rather than motivating
reparative action, shame often motivates denial, defensive anger
and aggression.*

— June Price Tangey (2000)

*What our healthy feeling of shame does is let us know that we are
limited. It tells us that to be human is to be limited. . . . Toxic shame
is no longer an emotion that signals our limits, it is a state of being,
a core identity. Toxic shame gives you a sense of worthlessness . . .
failing, falling short as a human being.*

— John Bradshaw (1998)

Like many feelings, shame can be an appropriate and even
helpful response on occasion, but if "overlearned" it can lead to
psychological and behavioral paralysis. As therapists, we need to
help our clients to distinguish between healthy and unhealthy
shame. Good shame helps us change. It is a temporary state of
mild to moderate discomfort based on that in us which is not our
better self. Without good shame, we are often doomed to repeat
inappropriate acts that harm others or ourselves. On the other
hand, unhealthy shame is toxic, leading us to doubt our every
action, our needs, and our drives. Whereas guilt can be useful in
constraining us from repeating actions that violate our personal
or cultural values, shame attacks our self-respect — our sense of
being a worthwhile human being.

The response to such corrosive feelings, according to June
Tangey's research on shame and guilt (2000), is an actual increase
in antisocial behavior and a decrease in self-esteem. The shamed

person is the poster child for negative self-talk: "I am defective," "I am incompetent," "I am unlovable" are their battle cries against themselves. These utterances often leave them paralyzed, unable to challenge their own recriminations, let alone the criticisms others may levy against them.

❖ A Case in Point

Julie was determined to be the mother her own mother never had been. From "Mommy and Me" classes when her son Tyler was three, to PTA president, to booster mother for Tyler's high school athletic teams, Julie was as supportive and involved as one could hope for. In spite of this, when Tyler graduated high school he went through a period of emotional turmoil and drug addiction. When this happened, Julie herself needed therapy to deal with her deep feelings of shame. "I questioned everything I had done as a parent. Was I too lenient, too strict, too involved, not involved enough. Was it the divorce? Should I have tried longer to make the marriage work? I was a ball of shame, a failure as a mother." Julie's shame had paralyzed and demoralized her.

❖ Putting It into Practice

Help clients understand that feelings of shame are a part of themselves that they must recognize. In the literature on treatment for shame, this is known as the "understanding stage" of therapy. If we help our clients recognize when they are reacting "shamefully," they can learn to catch themselves and learn to respond in a more self-supportive manner to criticism from self and others.

> *It is far better to befriend our shame than to treat it with dread or hatred. We must respect every part of ourselves, including our shame, to discover our love of ourselves.*
>
> — Patricia & Ronald Potter-Efron (1999)

Help clients to recognize the defenses they utilize to avoid the pain of shame. These defenses minimize immediate pain at the cost of ignoring reality. Withdrawal, rage, perfectionism, and arrogance are all attempts to stave off the inner shame. Insight into the use of these defenses can help clients develop alternative and more productive responses to such feelings.

The goal here is to understand how we protect ourselves from painful shame feelings and thoughts, not just to get rid of our defenses. Eventually, we will be able to make choices about how to live.

— Elizabeth Horst (1998)

Help clients to gently but firmly challenge their shameful beliefs about themselves. In this "action stage," we help clients to recognize their right to feel good about themselves and to receive respectful treatment from others and themselves and to see themselves as having value.

Prepare clients to spend many hours in animated discussion with their shameful self as it tries to convince them that they deserve to feel ashamed. Remind them that the most shamed of us have to commit themselves to the goal of self-worth over and over before it becomes comfortable.

— Judith Beck (1995)

❖ *The Option of Forgiveness*

Researchers and clinicians have more and more been investigating the possible therapeutic value of acts of forgiveness. For example, recent studies have found that a forgiveness protocol was effective for those having experienced sexual abuse and also in less traumatic but nonetheless upsetting relational problems.

— Nathaniel Wade et al. (2005)

There is a decided paradoxical quality to forgiveness, as the forgiver gives up the resentment to which he or she has a right, and gives the gift of compassion, to which the offender has no right.

— Suzanne Freedman and Robert Enright (1996)

As we reach out to the ones who hurt us, we are the ones that heal.

— Beverly Flanigan (1992)

We know that acts of injustice can never be forgotten, but can they and should they sometimes be forgiven? More and more researchers and clinicians are beginning to recognize that forgiveness can be a choice for clients who cannot let go of unrelenting anger and distress when other approaches to therapy have not been able to resolve the problem.

❖ A Case in Point

The news coverage was extensive. Amy Biehl, a twenty-three-year-old California woman who had journeyed to South Africa to help in that country's first "'all-race" elections, had been murdered by radical members of a black political party. After many months in which a powerful desire for vengeance was present, her parents made a decision to take positive action by establishing a foundation in their daughter's name, an organization devoted to her goals of peace and equal opportunity. As an act of forgiveness, they allowed two of the men who were involved in Amy's murder to work for the foundation following their release from prison.

Working with clients who have been victimized, we must recognize that they do not easily arrive at a place where they consider the possibility of forgiveness as a means of coping with their emotional pain. Rather, it is hard and sometimes painful work, involving patient and supportive guidance from the therapist. As with many psychological journeys, the road to forgiveness is one in which the client moves through successive stages of healing.

❖ Putting It into Practice

The task of the therapist in the first stage is to clearly acknowledge the injustice of what has befallen the client. In this stage, we fully join the client as someone who has been wronged and encourage the venting of feelings associated with the incident.

Here we help clients look at the walls they have built to protect themselves from feelings of anger and injustice. We begin to help them look over these walls and see the anger, and all its consequences.

— Robert Enright (2001)

In the next stage, the therapist helps the client recognize how ongoing feelings of rage and a desire for revenge may be negatively affecting the mind, body, and spirit, compounding the damage done by the original incident. We can then offer the option of forgiveness as a means to free them from the effects of negative experiences.

Surrendering the right to revenge can be equated to surrendering the right to carry the weight of the world on your back.

— Lewis Smedes (1996)

In the final stage, the therapist can encourage the client to engage in a number of cognitive and behavioral interventions, such as these suggested by Patton (1985):

❖ Putting aside claims to revenge against the perpetrator.

❖ Developing a fuller understanding of the perpetrator's background and motivation, which could have contributed to the abhorrent action. (This action is not undertaken to justify or condone the behavior, but simply to expand the client's perspective.)

❖ Dealing constructively with the pain — as in the case of the parents of Amy Biehl who transformed their anguish into a living legacy of their daughter.

❖ Being willing to allow the process of forgiveness to work itself out over time and not trying to control the process.

The Art of Healing:
The Debates

Ask four psychologists their position on a clinical issue and you will receive five different responses.

— Anonymous

I s briefer always better when it comes to therapy? When, if ever, should a therapist reveal personal experiences, flaws, or conflicts? Is there ever a proper time for therapists to give straightforward advice? What about strict allegiance to science vs. the use of one's intuition? Even with strict allegiance to a therapeutic approach, there are a number of philosophical and "process" variables that can fall through the cracks of our training, requiring that we invent our own school of thought, our own therapeutic model.

❖ Advice Giving

Advice is more agreeable in the mouth than in the ear.

— Mason Cooley (1996)

The therapist . . . deliberately does not intervene to solve the patient's problems or even advise the patient to proceed in a particular direction. He or she avoids recommending what actions to take, however tempting this may be, such as persuading a patient to dissolve a troubled marriage, encouraging him or her to quit a job or be more assertive.

— T. Byram Karasu (1992)

Either therapists can successfully influence behavior or they cannot, and they have little choice of what to claim.... If they wish to say that they cannot do so, or may do so in just those areas where human concern is greatest, and are therefore not at all responsible for the behavior of their clients, one must ask what right they have to be in business.

— Perry London (1964)

It has been accepted dogma since the time of the father of psychoanalysis, Sigmund Freud, that therapists should avoid like the plague giving direct advice to clients. After all, our clients have heard solicited and unsolicited guidance from friends, family, and the host of the psychology TV show, Dr. Phil, long before they came to therapy. However, some clinicians take this to an extreme and even if begged will not offer their personal guidance on a matter. On the other hand, there are those therapists who can't resist any opportunity to provide the solutions to clients' problems. Like so many things in life, advice giving involves a search for that middle ground — where we avoid taking responsibility for the client's life but do point out alternatives and give insights on why previous approaches might have failed.

❖ Cases in Point

Two women with similar problems initiate therapy with two different clinicians. Both are in their sixties, living in marriages that ran out of gas before they left the station. Both complain endlessly to their therapists about their miserable husbands. (It is not clear who is suffering more, the wives or the therapists.)

Dr. Pruitt becomes frustrated about the lack of progress and states firmly, "Because you are so unhappy and there seems to be no resolution, you need to leave for your own mental health." The client does in fact leave, but because of her high level of dependency begins to panic, calls the therapist daily, and becomes angry if not contacted immediately. She then tries to return to her husband, but he has moved on. Do you smell a lawsuit?

Dr. Wheelwright takes a different tack. Instead of a frontal assault, she helps her client generate a list of alternative actions, including doing nothing different, doing nothing different about the marriage but talking about it less in therapy sessions, doing nothing different about the marriage but talking about it more in sessions, and doing nothing different about the marriage but developing more independent activities. Perhaps out of compassion for Dr. Wheelwright, the client begins to invest more time in volunteer activities and developing social supports. Not a cure for the marriage, but both therapist and client improved.

❖ Putting It into Practice

Consider very carefully the temptation to give good advice, even when apparently agreeable clients ask you to.

I hate it when my clients ask me for advice. It's too tempting to take the bait and respond: "Well Sallie, I think you should keep busy and be nice to yourself." It isn't a bad answer. It's certainly well meaning. It's just unlikely to help.

— Suzanne Bender and Edward Messner (2003)

Ask yourself if are you willing to accept the consequences of what you are about to recommend if the client actually complies.

I cannot give advice. How can I when I do not authorize success.

— Gertrude Stein

Do not presume that because the recommended action has worked for you or others it is the best approach for your client.

To find a solution to his problems is up to the client; given perceptual freedom he may arrive at a very different resolution than what the therapist might have worked out for himself under similar circumstances.

— Michael Basch (1980)

❖ *Self-Disclosure vs. Professional Anonymity*

Self-disclosure can be used to create a more coequal relationship: it can communicate caring, encourage more open disclosures on the part of the client, acknowledge the therapeutic relationship as a fully human encounter, validate client experiences, and illustrate key points through personal examples.

— Sabert Basescu (1990)

If self-disclosure is not moderated, all the barriers between the personal and the professional become muddled. And the client's fundamental perceptions of therapist competence and empathy may be irrevocably altered.

— Jeffrey Kottler (2003)

The therapist conceals behind an impervious mask his or her private life, who he or she really is. Like the moon, the therapist reflects back . . . the patient's expectations of other people.

— Wayne Myers (1982)

Freudians say no to it: "It will ruin the blank screen upon which feelings can be projected and negate transference." Others object to it because exposing therapist weaknesses or vulnerabilities could reduce the client's trust in the therapist, adversely affecting treatment outcomes. A different perspective views appropriate self-disclosure as an opportunity to share with our clients our common humanity, a way of saying we have been there and done that — and survived. Of course, as in the rest of life, there can be too much of a good thing. We must avoid the trap of sharing too much information about too many things. We must be careful not to use self-disclosure as a way to self-glorify, meeting our own needs to appear heroic at the expense of the goals of therapy.

❖ Case in Point

A client asked a therapist who specialized in custody evaluations whether she had children herself. Having been trained to avoid self-disclosure at all costs, she tap-danced around the issue by suggesting that the more important issue was that she had conducted dozens of such evaluations and was known as a fair and thorough evaluator. Instead of responding positively to her deflection of the question, the client bolted and demanded that her lawyer find a different evaluator — one who was "not afraid to respond like a human being instead of hiding behind her professional role."

Remember, self-disclosure can be a potent therapeutic tool — leading to positive outcomes when used correctly.

Clients whose therapists engage in reciprocal self-disclosure (disclosures that match the clients' topic and intensity) show greater improvement and higher bonding to their therapists.

— Marna Barrett and Jeff Berman (2001)

Realize that certain types of self-disclosure are safer than others. Safe disclosures include:

❖ The therapist's professional experience and special training that bear on the specifics of the client's problems.
❖ The therapist's immediate emotional responses within the therapy session, such as mild to moderate feelings of frustration or boredom.

Avoid self-disclosures that are less safe such as:

❖ Those that are too personal in nature, for example: "Like you, I am going through a divorce currently."
❖ Those that are too intense compared to the client's disclosure, e.g., "I too had conflicts with my father, and ultimately I ended the relationship." — Barry Farber et al. (1996)

❖ *Empirical vs. Intuitive Therapy*

Empirical science is apt to cloud the sight, and, by the very knowledge of functions and processes, to bereave the student of the manly contemplation of the whole.

— Ralph Waldo Emerson (1849)

In a survey of mental health clinicians, the practice of keeping up with current clinical research was rated as the LOWEST of professional priorities.

— C. Edward Watkins and Lawrence Schneider (1991)

Perhaps the best piece of advice I received was from a supervisor during one of my internship rotations at a day hospital in London. "Be yourself," he said, "but examine your feelings." In other words, don't be a slave to some strict theory, don't just go by the book, trust your intuition but not without questioning it, and remember to keep your brain in gear.

— Arnold Lazarus (1997)

As the human brain evolved, we developed the capacity to respond rationally as well as emotionally. We can see this duality in various approaches to doing therapy as well. There are the strict "empiricists," who rely solely on well-researched (rational) models of therapy, and the "intuits," who are guided largely by gut-level feelings. Rather than an "either/or" approach, optimal therapy integrates the intuitive and the emotional, the tried and true with the spontaneous. Perhaps the difference between the two is that science accumulates knowledge, whereas intuition either repeats it or contests it.

❖ Case in Point

Sometimes what you see is not what you get, and this was the case with fifty-nine-year-old Alfonso. He told his therapist that he needed assistance adding novelty to his sex life with his new girlfriend, Beverly, because she seemed bored with him sexually. His previous relationships had all been "flings," whereas he viewed his new girlfriend as the "real thing." He concluded that Bev's apparent "boredom" with him was result of the fact that he had never been in a long-term relationship, and thus had never really learned the art of lovemaking. Something didn't sound right about all of this — Alfonso loved Beverly, and she told him she loved him as well. Was sexual novelty so necessary for Bev? Intuitively, the therapist thought the answer lay elsewhere, and when he brought this up to the couple in a joint session, Beverly confessed that sex for her had never been pleasing, and that, in fact, she didn't even like being touched. In a heartbeat, the case went from sexual enhancement therapy for Alfonso to sex abuse recovery for Beverly.

❖ Putting It into Practice

Consider the possibility that there is a place in the therapeutic arsenal for both intuitive approaches and those that are based on empirical evidence.

Creativity in therapy is seldom the result of emotion solely. It is fueled by emotion, sometimes guided by intuition, but is built upon a knowledge base that allows something new to be created from something old.

— Ellen Levine (2004)

Relying on empirical evidence requires that clinicians allot sufficient time to review journals or academic databases to stay up on current research.

The great tragedy of science — the slaying of a beautiful theory by an ugly fact.
— Thomas Henry Huxley (1870)

Relying on our intuition requires that we "get in touch with our feelings," something we often tell our clients to do while, perhaps, neglecting this maxim ourselves.

Science is facts. Just as houses are made of stones, so is science made of facts. But a pile of stones is not a house and a collection of facts is not necessarily science.
— Jules Henri Poincare (1914)

On Healing in a "Briefer-the-Better" HMO World

❖

The very nature of many brief, manualized and/or medical interventions does not allow for extended periods of empathic listening, listening that allows clients to reveal rather than state their concerns. Instead, clients are forced by the pace and focus of such treatments, often in their first session, to describe themselves and their problems as if they knew and understood both in their entirety.
— Steven Graybar and Leah Leonard (2005)

On close examination the research support for time limits vanishes, and the actual research evidence shows that time limits are harmful. The belief that research supports time limits has only survived because the evidence was never closely scrutinized.
— Ronald Miller (2005)

Clients who were seen for a SINGLE SESSION have done as well as those who stayed for a longer course of therapy.
— (our emphasis) Michael Hoyt et al. (1992)

It seems that the pendulum has swung from viewing therapy as a life-long pursuit (the Woody Allen syndrome) to the opposite extreme, where briefer is better and briefest is best (the HMO syndrome). Certainly, some studies (Bloom, Yeager & Roberts, 2006; Basoglu, Livanou & Salcioglu, 2003) have shown that brief therapies have been effectively applied to a number of presenting problems; however, in these cases, most often the therapist and client agreed on the length of treatment. That scenario is a far cry from the current situation in which managed care imposes time limits, incentives for short-term treatment, or both. The battle lines have been drawn, with clinicians emphasizing the client's treatment needs and HMOs all too often focusing on the economic bottom line.

❖ A Case in Point

Adjusting to divorce can often be a tricky affair, but for Peter, aged forty-three, it was particularly difficult given his considerable success in business and a history of independent problem solving. Now he needed help dealing with the fact that "Mr. Success" had been left by his wife of twelve years for another man. The diagnosis sent to the insurance carrier was "adjustment disorder, with anxiety," and it approved a limited number of sessions. Unfortunately, just as Peter made progress, a contentious custody battle ensued and his mother broke her hip, initiating a family war over who should be financially responsible — two steps forward, one and a half steps back. All of this happened just as the approved number of sessions was ending. The insurance carrier resisted attempts to provide ongoing therapy on the grounds that the diagnosis was not severe enough to warrant it. Effectively, the insurance carrier was asking for a more severe diagnosis, when in fact one stress after another was hitting Peter; a far more common problem than bureaucracies seem to admit.

❖ Putting It into Practice

Do not be discouraged by having to learn short-term therapy techniques. Using them is not second class, a cop out, or pandering to business interests.

Short-term therapy has been mistakenly believed to be synonymous with managed care (the limiting of treatment by insurance company protocols), but the two are in fact not connected in their origins. . . . Research on short term therapy began in the late 1970s, because of an interest in learning how to make therapy as efficient and effective as possible.

— Leigh McCullough (2005)

Views of Human Nature

Psychology keeps trying to vindicate human nature. History keeps undermining the effort.

— Mason Cooley (1996)

Our tacit assumptions about human nature unquestionably influence how we view and serve individuals who seek psychological services.

— Michael Mahoney (2005)

My experience is that [humankind] is basically trustworthy, tending toward development, differentiation, cooperative relationships.

— Carl Rogers (1961)

A new client arrives. What are our expectations? Do we have a pure "wait and see" attitude? What kind of human will darken our door? (Or "lighten our door"?) Of course, we expect clients to be troubled in one way or another, but beyond their symptoms, do we tend to expect clients to be trustworthy, changeable, complex, and altruistic, or do we expect the opposite? What we believe about human nature has no small effect on the outcome of therapy. For example, those clinicians who believe that human beings cannot change significantly, that our nature is "fixed" permanently, may find a self-fulfilling prophecy in which pessimism breeds modest expectations for therapist and client alike. In practice, lowered expectations about clients such as sex offenders, recalcitrant substance abusers, and others who come to therapy involuntarily has been shown to dramatically affect therapeutic outcome (Noonan, 1998, Duckro, 1991). Abraham Maslow (1991), the father of humanism in psychology, put it this way:

Every psychologist . . . has a full blown philosophy of human nature hidden away within him . . . this unconscious theory guides his reactions far more than does his laboriously acquired experimental knowledge.

❖ A Case in Point

Vishwa, aged fifty, had been through this many times before: admission to the county hospital, a twelve-step program, the hunt for root causes, the self-management program. Dr. Goya had about as much faith that treatment would work as Vishwa did. Unfortunately, he had read the statistics about relapsers, and, in general, had a view of human nature that held that people really don't change all that much. After starting down the same well-worn therapeutic path that others had tried, Dr. Goya decided to switch to a focus on the longest period of time during which Vishwa had attained sobriety. Dissecting this period revealed that Vishwa started to fall off the wagon not because "that's what relapsers do" but because marital stress had built up, and he had not acted as swiftly as in the past to resolve the issues. Second, he had reduced his contact with his Alcoholic Anonymous sponsor, thinking he had made sufficient progress to go it alone. Once Vishwa recognized the triggers for relapse, he had a better sense of what he needed to do to remain sober. Vishwa felt more optimistic about his treatment, and Dr. Goya started to question his negative bias about the ability of even chronic alcoholics to make real change. Vishwa remained sober for the next twenty-seven years until his passing.

❖ Putting It into Practice

Assess your assumptions about human nature to better understand how your personal beliefs can affect your therapeutic work. The following questions from Wrightsman (1992) can help you explore your beliefs about key dimensions of human nature:

❖ Trustworthiness: Do you believe that most people are basically honest?

❖ Strength of will: Do you believe that if a person tries hard enough he will probably reach his goals?

❖ Altruism: Do you believe that most people do not hesitate to go out of their way to help another person?

❖ Independence: Do you believe that most people can make decisions uninfluenced by what others may think of that decision?

❖ Complexity: Do you believe that people are so complex that it is hard to know what makes them tick?

Recognize the inherent potential for good and evil within all of us.

I propose the evil in our culture is also a reflection of the evil in ourselves. The culture is evil as well as good because we, the human beings who constitute it, are evil as well as good.

— Rollo May (1989)

VIII

Evolving Perspectives on Therapy

T he field of psychotherapy has never been and probably never will be a static one. Many of Freud's initial followers (Carl Jung, Alfred Adler, etc.) bent, folded, and stapled his ideas, introducing new concepts and dimensions to his framework. Even Freud himself became a Neo-Freudian over time, revising and modifying his original ideas. This evolution of psychotherapy continues unabated today, incorporating insights from such fields as neurobiology, Eastern philosophy, and developmental psychology. These insights have greatly expanded our options as healers and illuminated new and innovative ways of looking at clinical work. Hopefully, none of us is doing therapy the same way we did it ten years ago or the way we will do it ten years hence, as the field continues to make advances.

❖ *The Neurobiological View of Therapy*

When psychotherapy results in symptom reduction or experiential change, the brain has, in some way, been altered.

— Eric Kandel (2005)

The inner menagerie of the three brains, (reptilian, paelomammalian and neomammalian) confronts the therapist with the challenge of treating a human, a horse and a crocodile.

— Charles Hampden-Turner (1971)

*Vast reductions in the degree of physical activity required to obtain
necessary resources in today's society likely lead to reduced activation of
brain areas essential for reward/pleasure, motivation, problem-solving,
and effective coping strategies (i.e., depressive symptomatology).*

— Kelly Lambert (2005)

What goes on inside the brain when psychotherapy induces
change and healing in an individual? Neuroscientists have begun to
understand the complex interaction between "change experiences"
and brain function. This is quite revolutionary given the history
of psychiatry, which for decades classified emotional illnesses as an
either/or phenomenon: either the disorder was organic, or it was
the result of functional or social factors.

The current view is that all mental processes are biological and
therefore any change in these processes is necessarily organic.
Neuroscience has determined that a number of disorders,
including depression and anxiety, involve impaired neurological
function. For example, in anxiety disorders, the cortical networks
responsible for memory, language, and integration are affected.
In depression, there are actual losses of neurons in the areas
connecting the prefrontal cortex and the limbic system.
Psychotherapy, from a neuroscientist's perspective, addresses
these deficits by providing an enriched environment capable of
enhancing the growth of neurons and the integration of neural
networks. This new and revolutionary conceptualization offers an
optimistic view of the potential of psychotherapy to change our
clients at both the functional and organic levels.

❖ A Case in Point

Louis Cozolino, in his book *The Neuroscience of Psychotherapy*
(2003), describes a middle-aged woman who complained of severe
memory problems, particularly those involving names, dates, and
appointments. These difficulties affected her relationships and job
aspirations. Her history included numerous traumas and stressors
in early childhood. Several therapists had given up on her because
she repeatedly missed or was late to sessions. They viewed her
lateness as a defensive style of denial and repression. Cozolino,
instead, utilized his perspective as a neuroscientist and posited that

the client's memory problems were the result of the destructive role of "early and prolonged stress on the development of the neural networks" that organize the types of explicit memory (names, dates, etc.) with which she was having trouble.

The initial stages of therapy, therefore, addressed "neurological retraining" in which the therapist provided the client with various memory aids (a daytimer, a watch with alarms, computer programs) and activities designed to "exercise her memory." After six weeks, she was consistently able to remember appointments, and therapy shifted to the impact of her life experiences on her relationships and career.

❖ Putting It into Practice

Recognize that although therapy is not brain surgery, appropriate therapeutic interventions do in fact alter brain function and structure.

After treatment for OCD with a combination of mindfulness and refocusing, the right caudate nucleus, responsible in part for the worry circuit, actually diminished in size and activity. Perhaps the pejorative term for psychologists — "shrink" — is sometimes appropriately descriptive.

— Jeffrey Schwartz and Sharon Begley (2003)

Help clients understand that even though both medication and psychotherapy can enhance brain function, the effects of psychotherapy can be longer lasting.

When compared to psychotherapy, pharmacotherapy has a major disadvantage in that relapse rates are higher after drug therapy termination than therapy.

— Bernard Beitman and Yue Dongmei (2004)

Promote the idea to clients that whatever their genetic heritage or life experiences, our brains are plastic enough to adapt and generate life-enhancing neurological connections.

It is not a matter of nature versus nurture, it is that nature needs nurture.

— Marion Solomon and Daniel Siegel (2003)

❖ Mindfulness: The Eastern View

To be mindful is to wake up — to recognize what is happening in the present moment, our attention is not entangled in the past or future and we are not judging or rejecting what is occurring at the moment.

— Christopher Germer et al. (2005)

The here-and-now is the major source of therapeutic power, the pay dirt of therapy, the therapist's (and hence the patient's) best friend.

— Irvin Yalom (2003)

You finally figure out that it's only the clock that's going around. It's doing its thing, but you — you're sitting here right now always.

— Ram Dass (1971)

The world is truly shrinking. There is an integration of cultures occurring that pervades many realms of our lives: the global economy, world music, fusion cuisine — and in the realm of healing, the blending of Western and Eastern medicine and psychotherapies. "Mindfulness" is the Western term for the state of mind in which we pay attention in the present — nonjudgmentally. It is the opposite of mindlessness, a state in which we:

Rush through activities without attentiveness
Forget people's names almost as soon as we have heard it
Break or spill things due to carelessness
Do not notice subtle feelings of physical tension or discomfort
Snack without being aware of eating
Preoccupy ourselves with the past and future.

— Jon Kabat-Zinn (1994)

Don't feel bad if you recognize yourself on that list of inattentive behaviors. It seems to perfectly encapsulate our contemporary mode of living — or should it be called "existing"?

When we are mindful, we are engaged in the present, not entangled in the past, not rejecting what is occurring. The result is that we are freer, more alive, more energized, more clearheaded.

There are a number of studies indicating that mindfulness training is a promising adjunct to therapy with a number of diagnoses, including chronic pain and borderline personality disorder.

❖ A Case in Point

Tara Bennet-Goleman, in her book *Emotional Alchemy* (2002), describes a case in which mindfulness was a useful adjunct to therapy. The client, Maya, battled chronic ulcerative colitis. To add to her physical problems she tended to overeat — all the wrong kinds of foods. She began practicing mindfulness at times when she felt like binging — simply observing all the sensations, thoughts, and feelings in her mind and body. Over time, she came to realize that she tended to binge when she felt unloved — and that she had had such feelings from very early in her life. This insight led her to seek nurturance in more healthy ways, and her intense cravings for food began to dissolve.

❖ Putting It into Practice

Mindfulness, when applied to the therapeutic relationship, involves a pattern of nonpossessiveness and kindness based in the three As of caring: attention, acceptance, and appreciation. David Richo describes these in his book, *How to Be an Adult in Relationships* (2002).

Pay attention. As therapists, we are mindful when we pay attention compassionately to our own thoughts, feelings, and responses, as well as to the client's.

. . . not dispassionately, not standing aloof — but standing by.

Show acceptance.

By accepting and not judging our clients, we make room for them to be who they are.

Demonstrate appreciation. When we praise or show delight in our clients, it gives depth to our expression of acceptance.

Words of admiration, respect, and liking are the foundation of all relationships including those that are therapeutic.

❖ The Constructivist View

It is in changing that things find repose.

— Heraclitus (circa 500 B.C.E.)

The primary purpose of psychotherapy, from a constructivist perspective, is to provide compassionate encouragement and professional counsel as individuals work to reorganize themselves and their lives.

— Michael Mahoney (2003)

New avenues of behavior open themselves to a person when he reconstrues the course of events surrounding him. Thus a thoughtful person is neither the prisoner of his environment nor the victim of his biography.

— George Kelly (1963)

The verb "to construct" means to organize or create order. In constructive psychology, we human beings are seen as actively constructing our view of reality, our sense of ourselves, our values, and our sense of control. In this view, we are neither spectators nor mere pawns in our lives. Constructivism is predicated on five themes: (1) active agency, (2) order, (3) self, (4) social-symbolic relatedness, and (5) lifespan development. Together, then, the constructivist view of human experience is one that emphasizes "actions aimed at making sense of the world by a developing self in relation to others" (Mahoney, 2003). The underpinnings of constructivism are ancient, ranging from Taoism and Buddhism and continuing to the modern age with the personal, social, and narrative emphases of contemporary constructivists like Bandura, Bruner, Kelly, Gergen, and Mahoney.

As long as our ordering processes keep us balanced in life, we thrive. However, life is change and often we experience challenges to our equilibrium — challenges that require that we change our personal constructs, our core views of our selves. This process can be overwhelming because to reorganize we must first face and endure disorganization of what we previously held dear. Thus, those who come to us for counseling are often seeking to regain a sense of order, meaning, or balance in their lives.

In a "constructive" approach to therapy, clients set the pace of their therapy, allowing time for them to integrate new ways of acting and thinking. The pioneer of constructivism, Jean Piaget, referred to this integration of the new as "assimilation" and "accommodation" — processes in which either we shape new information to fit existing concepts or the new information causes modification of those concepts. The time needed for such reflection, of course, runs counter to the "drive-through" philosophy of therapy in the age of HMOs.

Constructive therapists are also concerned with providing safety and only as much structure as the client requires. This construct is similar to the idea of "scaffolding" developed by the developmental psychologist L.S. Vygotsky, wherein teachers and parents present and support challenges that are just outside a child's comfort zone. Thus therapy is seen as a venue for attempting new explorations and experiments, with the therapist supplying the safety net to ensure that reasonable risks are undertaken.

One method of applying constructivism involves Kelly's (1963) technique known as "fixed role therapy." In this method we ask the client to act out in everyday life the role of someone who thinks and acts differently. As the client experiments with new ways of being and "construing," she or he has opportunities to incorporate new perspectives into the sense of self.

❖ A Case in Point

Maria complained that the new CEO was the "boss from hell," the complete opposite of her previous boss, who treated her respectfully and valued her feedback and opinions. Now she was being treated like a mere "gopher," fetching coffee and entertaining his young children when they visited. She felt trapped into the job because there was no other position in the organization and she was close to being vested for retirement. As the months progressed, Maria alternated between depression and uncontrollable anger — resulting in outbursts that led to reprimands and threats of termination. She entered therapy somewhat reluctantly, feeling that the problem was her boss' not hers, and that she was simply responding like anyone in her position would. Of interest to the therapist was the fact that

Maria had been practicing yoga for several years and had attended workshops with renowned yogis from India, as well as the Dalai Lama. With this in mind, the therapist suggested Kelly's fixed role approach, which would involve having her act with her boss as the Dalai Lama would under similar circumstances. This meant assuming more of an accepting, compassionate, and patient mode of behavior. Obviously, this would be a big stretch for Maria, so at first the goal was to have her do so for only fifteen minutes a day. This approach did not come easy for Maria, and some days she just could not muster up the necessary "Zen-like" attitude. However, gradually, the relationship improved. As Maria became more tolerant, there was less acrimony and polarization. The CEO did not become the boss of her dreams; he still excluded her from higher-level decision making, but Maria's mood improved significantly and she was able to remain in her position until she was fully vested in her retirement fund.

Remember that our clients (and we) construct reality through the lenses they (and we) use to view the world. If we can provide them with new lenses, we can help clients reconstruct their world.

When I was nine years old, living in a ghetto township in South Africa...I read a tattered issue of Ebony *magazine that had on its cover a picture of Jackie Robinson, who had just broken the race barrier in baseball. For me it was an incredible sort of fresh air — I had always been told there was a ceiling above which I could not go, and here was a guy who had broken through that ceiling — it gave me a new view of what was possible.*

— Desmond Tutu (2000)

Applying constructivism to therapy involves making the clients' "meaning system" superior to the therapist's theoretical orientation or personal beliefs.

Constructivism provides a strong rationale for respecting the preeminence of the client's worldview.... It emphasizes the client's idiosyncratic meaning system as the impetus for therapy.

— Peter Salovey (2003)

Help clients expand their views of their problems and life situations using narratives, metaphors, and puzzles. Milton Erickson, known for his extensive use of metaphor and study in psychotherapy, used this approach to great effect as the following story demonstrates:

Once Erickson described the layout of a house and asked his students how many ways they could get into the master bedroom. After the students would exhaust the conventional, pedestrian ways, he would suggest that one could drive to the airport, take a plane to a different city, a train back, and then a taxi to the house and enter through a window.

— Michael Hoyt (2000)

❖ *Resource-Based Therapy*

Clients bring into therapy the resources that are necessary to resolve their complaints. Therapy helps them to find these resources within themselves.

— Steve de Shazer (1985)

We don't need to uncover all our sadness in order to experience happiness. We don't need to discuss hate in order to develop love. We don't need to talk about problems in order to find viable solutions. We only need to pay more attention and practice more of what we wish to accomplish.

— Moshe Talmon (1990)

Successful therapists . . . tend to have developed an unshakeable belief that somewhere in their clients' recent history there are life experiences manifesting fragments of ability, competence or talent that the client is not presently able to notice or apply to their concerns.

— Gerald Monk et al. (1996)

In the past, most therapeutic approaches have operated on a "deficiency" model, that is, a client is someone who is lacking in certain mental health fundamentals. These deficits come in all shapes and sizes: not recognizing one's inner conflicts and related defenses; using faulty, distorted, or irrational thinking styles; or lacking specific behavioral skills. However, more recently, there has been an emphasis on client strengths as well as the obstacles that cause pain, conflict, or dilemmas. Moshe Talmon (1990) has labeled this new synthesis "therapy in a new key."

Three pillars support this positive perspective. The first is the concept of "psychohealth" in which client resources or strengths are assessed as adequately as their deficits. Second, a "solutions approach" is used in which client successes in the past are adapted to present difficulties. Last, therapy is seen as a "partnership" as opposed to a hierarchal process in which the therapist is the "sage on the stage." Narrative therapists such as Gerald Monk et al. (1996) also emphasize strengths while helping clients to create a future life story in which current problems have been resolved.

❖ Cases in Point

A former track star turned motivational speaker freezes during a presentation and cannot face another audience. She is encouraged to visualize her successful return several years prior to athletic competition after recovering from a serious injury.

A male nurse who was sexually harassed by his superior is afraid to testify against her in court. The therapist helps him to remember previous acts of courage, including leaving his family in South America and journeying to the United States.

A socially phobic young man terrified of giving a speech in his communications class recalls his "glory days" in high school quarterbacking the football team. He delivers a talk on the role of sports in developing character and uses a football as a prop — and a reminder of how he was able to perform in front of a stadium full of fans.

❖ Putting It into Practice

A full history takes into account the clients' accomplishments, interests, and obstacles that have been overcome.

Understanding positive individual traits consists of the study of strengths and virtues: the capacity for love and work, courage, compassion, resilience, creativity, curiosity, integrity, self-knowledge, moderation, self-control, and wisdom.

— Martin Seligman (2006)

Recognize that mental health is much more than merely eliminating personal suffering.

True therapy also involves the enhancement of positive emotions, finding activities that help activate engagement or flow, and finding commitments and connections in life beyond oneself, such as political, religious or charitable involvements.

— Christopher Peterson (2006)

Help clients focus on a future in which the presenting problem has been resolved.

We are natural storytellers, so why not create our own story — one in which we visualize taking the steps to a fulfilling future, in which we have overcome current problems through corrective action?

— Gerald Monk et al. (1996)

After-Thoughts

And so the field of psychotherapy continues to evolve. In its one hundred or so years of existence, we have seen many shifts in clinical focus. First, we explored the unconscious world of repressed emotions, then we modified behaviors — then cognitions — then both behaviors and cognitions. Then it was back to a focus on unconscious emotions which needed reprocessing. Then the field expanded to include a more global perspective on mental health, incorporating elements of eastern philosophy, such as mindfulness and acceptance. The "final" frontier is now being investigated as clinicians have been attempting to unify all these disparate modalities into an "integrative psychology."

Throughout this shifting of theoretical sands, the recycling, the innovations, one factor has remained constant — the force of the therapeutic relationship. Yet even that has been tested. For a brief moment some clever computer programmers thought you might be able to bypass a living breathing therapist with software that simulated the human factor. The "client," seated at a computer, was asked a series of questions and — voilà! — all possible human travail was neatly addressed and remediated. One can only marvel at the audacity of those behind this short-lived notion that the human condition is reducible to a determinable number of binary permutations. Will online counseling meet a similar fate, or can enough human contact be garnered through email correspondence to develop a therapeutic bond? Only time will tell.

The most recent challenge to the person-to-person aspect of doing therapy arises from the new world of looming bureaucracies which ask us not only to heal, but to do so rapidly.

"Briefer is better" — and "briefest is best" — seem to be the operating principles of many "health" maintenance organizations. (If only "health" were their main consideration!) With such pressures upon clinicians, perhaps it is appropriate to end our short review of reflections on therapeutic healing with a few reminders of the primacy of the human connection:

The complexity of human change requires us to acknowledge that deeper forces are at work, processes within each client that are ignited by connections with the therapist.

— Jeffrey Kottler

In order for the process of mutual influence to unfold, the therapist must "show up" in relationships as an authentic presence and open him or herself to the possibility of healing and change.

— Maureen Walker

Only connect . . .

— E.M. Forster

Suggested Readings

Ashelman, K. A., Marks, N.F., & Enright, R.D. (1997). *Forgiveness as a resiliency factor in divorced and permanently separated families.* Madison: University of Wisconsin.

Benedek, F. (1952). Infertility as a psychosomatic defense. *Fertility and Sterility, 3,* 527–541.

Brown, B. (2000). *1001 motivational messages and quotations for athletes and coaches: Teaching character through sport.* Monterey, CA: Coaches Choice Books.

Chamy, I. (1999). Courage and yielding in the Holocaust. *Advances in Mind-Body Medicine, 15,* 65–68.

Clynes, M., & Panskepp, J. (1988). *Emotions, brain, immunity, and health: A review. Emotions and psychopathology.* New York: Plenum Press.

Dreyfus, H. L., & Dreyfus, S. E. (1986). *Mind over machine.* New York: Free Press.

Eisendrath, P., & Widemann, F. (1987). *Female authority: Empowering women through psychotherapy.* New York: Guilford Press.

Epstein, L. (1977). The therapeutic function of hate in the counter-transference. *Contemporary Psychoanalysis, 13,* 442–461.

Fossumm, M., & Mason, M. (1989). *Facing shame.* New York: W.W. Norton & Company.

Frankl, V. (1984). *Man's search for meaning.* New York: Touchstone.

Glasser, W. (1996). I can't wait until you leave. In J. A. Kottler, & J. Carlson (Eds.), *Bad therapy: Master therapists share their worst failures.* New York: Brunner-Routledge.

Graybar, S., & Leonard, L. (2005). In defense of listening. *American Journal of Psychotherapy, 59*(1), 1–18.

Hickman, M. (1994). *Healing after loss: Daily meditations for working through grief.* New York: Avon Books.

Hicks, M. D. (1999). The development pipeline: How people really learn. *Knowledge Management Review, 9,* 30–33.

Hill, C. L., & Ridley, C. R. (2001). Diagnostic decision-making: Do counselors delay final judgments? *Journal of Counseling & Development, 9,* 98–118.

115

Jennings, L., Hanson, M., & Skovholt, T. (2005). Mastery and expertise in counseling. *Journal of Mental Health Counseling, 27*(1), 19–31.

Kissane, D.W., & Bloch, S. (2000). *Family focused grief therapy: A model of family-centered care during palliative care and bereavement.* Berkshire, United Kingdom: Open University Press.

Krzyzewski, M. (2000). *Leading with the heart.* South Victoria, Australia: Warner Books.

Levitt, E., & Lubin, B. (1967). Some personality factors associated with menstrual cycle complaints and menstrual attitudes. *Journal of Psychosomatic Research, 11,* 267–270.

McMahon, S. (1992). *The portable therapist: Wise and inspiring answers to the questions people in therapy ask the most.* New York: Dell Books.

Miller, S., Huble, M., & Duncan, B. (1996). *Handbook of solution-focused brief therapy.* San Francisco: Jossey-Bass.

Sacks, O. (1987). *The man who mistook his wife for a hat and other clinical tales.* New York: Summit Books (Simon & Schuster).

Siegel, S. (1993). *The patient who cured his therapist: And other stories of unconventional therapy.* New York: Plume Books.

Skinner, N. F. (2001). A course, a course, my kingdom for a course: Reflections of an unrepentant teacher. *Canadian Psychology, 42,* 49–60.

Strean, H. S. (2000). Sometimes I feel like a dirty old man: The woman who tried to seduce me. In I. Rabinowitz (Ed.), *Inside therapy: Illuminating writings about therapists, patients, and psychotherapy.* New York: St. Martin's Press.

Twemlow, S. (2001). Training psychotherapists in attributes of mind from Zen and psychoanalytic perspectives. Part I: Core principles, emptiness, impermanence and paradox. *American Journal of Psychotherapy, 55*(1), 1–21.

Weber, R., & Gans, J. (2003). The group therapist's shame: A much undiscussed topic. *International Journal of Group Psychotherapy, 53,* 395–416.

Wilhelm, S. (2006). *Cognitive therapy for obsessive compulsive disorder: A guide for professionals.* Oakland, CA: New Harbinger Publications.

Wrightsman, L. S. (1991). *Assumptions about human nature: Implications for researchers and practitioners.* Newbury Park, CA: Sage Publications.

References

Ainsworth, M., & Bowlby, J. (1953). *Child care and the growth of love*. New York: Penguin.

Allen, G. (1989). *Strategies for winning: A top coach's game plan for victory in football and in life*. New York: McGraw Hill.

Allen, W. (1982). Quoted in T.J. Peters & R.H. Waterman, *In search of excellence: Lessons from America's best-run companies*. New York: Harper & Row.

Anderson, S. (2000). *The journey from abandonment to healing: Turn the end of a relationship into the beginning of a new life*. New York: Berkley Publishing Group.

Aretino, P. (2005). *Aretino's dialogues*. Canada: University of Toronto Press.

Ausberger, D. (1980). *Caring enough to confront: How to understand and express your deepest feelings toward others*. Ventura, CA: Regal Books.

Bailey, C.E. (2005). *Children in therapy: Using the family as a resource*. New York: W.W. Norton.

Baranowsky, A., Gentry, J.E., & Schultz, D.F. (2005). *Trauma practice: Tools for stabilization and recovery*. Cambridge: Hogrefe & Huber.

Barrett, M., & Berman, J. (2001). Is psychotherapy more effective when psychotherapists disclose information about themselves? *Journal of Counseling and Clinical Psychology, 69*(4), 597–603.

Basch, M. (1980). *Doing psychotherapy*. New York: Basic Books.

Basescu, S. (1990). Tools of the trade: The use of self in psychotherapy. *Group, 14*, 157–165.

Basoglu, M., Livanou, M., & Salcioglu, E. (2003). A brief behavioural treatment of chronic post-traumatic stress disorder in earthquake survivors: Results from an open clinical trial. *Psychological Medicine, 33*(4), 647–654.

Batson, C., Thompson, E., Seuferling, G., Whitney, H., & Strongman, J. (1999). Moral hypocrisy: Appearing moral to oneself without being so. *Journal of Personality and Social Psychology, 77*(3), 525–537.

Battino, R. (2006). *Expectation: The very brief therapy book*. Williston, VT: Crown House Publishing.

Baumeister, R., DeWall, N., & Ciarocco, N. (2005). Social exclusion impairs self-regulation. *Journal of Personality and Social Psychology, 88*(4), 589–604.

Beck, A., Wright, F.D., Newman, C.F., & Liese, B.S. (2001). *Cognitive therapy of substance abuse.* New York: Guilford Press.

Beck, J. (1995). *Cognitive therapy: Basics and beyond.* New York: Guilford Press.

Bedell, J., & Lennox, S. (1997). *Handbook for communication and problem solving skills training: A cognitive behavioral approach.* New York: John Wiley & Sons.

Beitman, B., & Dongmei, Y. (2004). *Learning psychotherapy: A time-efficient, research-based, and outcome-measured psychotherapy training program.* New York: W.W. Norton.

Bender, S., & Messner, E. (2003). *Becoming a therapist: What do I say, and why?* New York: Guilford Press.

Benjamin, B., Marcus, S., & Cadwell, C. (1965). Please don't let me be misunderstood [The Animals]. On *Retrospective* [CD]. Philadephia: Abkco Records. (September 1969).

Bennet-Goleman, T. (2002). *Emotional alchemy: How the mind can heal the heart.* New York: Three Rivers Press.

Berg, B., & Rosenblum, N. (1977). Fathers in family therapy: A survey of family therapists. *Journal of Marital and Family Therapy, 3*(1), 85–91.

Berra, Y., & Kaplan, D. (2001). *When you come to a fork in the road, take it!: Inspiration and wisdom from one of baseball's greatest heroes.* Waterville, ME: Thorndike Press.

Bertolino, B., & Schultheis, G. (2002). *The therapist's notebook for families: Solution oriented exercises for working with parents, children and adolescents.* Binghamton, NY: Haworth Press.

Binder, J. (2004). *Key competencies in brief dynamic psychotherapy: Clinical practice beyond the manual.* New York: Guilford Press.

Bloom, B.L., Yeager, K.R., & Roberts, A.R. (2006). Evidence-based practice with anxiety disorders: Guidelines based on 59 outcome studies. In A.R. Roberts & K.R. Yeager (Eds.), *Foundations of evidence-based social work practice* (pp. 275–290). New York: Oxford University Press.

Bongers, M., de Winter, C.R., & Kompier, M.A. (1993). Psychosocial factors at work and musculoskeletal disease. *Scandinavian Journal of Work, Environment & Health, 19*(5), 297–312.

Booraem, C., Flowers, J., & Schwartz, B. (1992). Group therapy outcome and satisfaction as a function of the counselor's use of rapid assessment instruments. *Proceedings of the 1992 Western Psychological Association Convention.*

Bordin, E. (1994). Theory and research on the working alliance inventory: New directions. In L. Greenberg & A. Horvath (Eds.), *The working alliance, theory, research and practice* (pp. 13–17). New York: Wiley.

Bowlby, J. (1997). *Attachment and loss.* NewYork: Pimlico/Random House.

Boyd, B.A. (2002). Examining the relationship between stress and lack of social support in mothers of children with autism. *Focus on Autism and Other Developmental Disabilities, 17*(4), 208–215.

Bradshaw, J. (1988). *Healing the shame that binds you.* Deerfield Beach, FL: Health Communications.

Brady, J., Norcross, J., Guy, J., & Healy, F. (1995). Stress in counsellors. In W. Dryden (Ed.), *The stresses of counselling in action.* Newbury Park, CA: Sage Publications.

Briere, J., & Scott, C. (2006). *Principles of trauma therapy: A guide to symptoms, evaluation and treatment.* Newbury Park, CA: Sage Publications.

Burns, G. (2001). *101 healing stories: Using metaphor in therapy.* New York: W.W. Norton.

Butcher, J. (2002). *Clinical personality assessment: Practical approaches.* New York: Oxford University Press.

Carson, D., & Becker, K. (2003). *Creativity in psychotherapy: Reaching new heights with individuals.* Binghamton, NY: Haworth Press.

Castonguay, L., Goldfried, M., Wiser, S., Raue, P., & Hayes, A. (1996). Predicting the effect of cognitive therapy for depression: A study of unique and common factors. *Journal of Consulting and Clinical Psychology, 64*(3), 497–504.

Chekhov, A. (2004). *A life in letters.* (R. Bartlett, Ed., A. Phillips, Trans.). New York: Penguin Classics.

Chertok, L., Mondzain, M.L., & Bonnaud, M. (1963). Vomiting and the wish to have a child. *Psychosomatic Medicine, 25*(1), 13–18.

Chin, J., De La Cancela, V., & Jenkins, Y. (2003). *Diversity in psychotherapy: The politics of race, ethnicity and gender.* West Port, CT: Praeger Publishers.

Christensen, A., & Jacobson, N. (1998). *Acceptance and change in couple's therapy: A therapist's guide to transforming relationships.* New York: W.W. Norton.

Combs, G., & Freedman, J. (1990). *Symbol, story and ceremony.* New York: W.W. Norton.

Cooley, M. (1996). City aphorisms. *The Columbia World of Quotations.* Retrieved April 8, 2007, from http://www.bartleby.com/66/12/13412.html.

Cousins, N. (1989). *Head first: The biology of hope.* New York: Dutton.

Cozolino, L. (2003). *The neuroscience of psychotherapy.* New York: W.W. Norton.

Cross, D.G., & Warren, C.G. (1984). Environmental factors associated with continuers and terminators in adult outpatient psychotherapy. *British Journal of Medical Psychology, 57*(4), 363–369.

Cross, M. (2001). *Becoming a therapist: A manual for personal and professional development*. Philadelphia, PA: Brunner-Routledge.

Cross, P., & Steadman, M. (1996). *Classroom research: Implementing the scholarship of teaching*. San Francisco: Jossey-Bass.

Curry, J., Rohde, P., Simons, A., Silva, S., Vitiello, B., Kratochvil, C., et al. (2006). Predictors and moderators of acute outcome in the Treatment for Adolescents with Depression Study (TADS). *Journal of the American Academy of Child & Adolescent Psychiatry, 45*(12), 1427–1439.

Dacey, J., & Lennon, K. (1998). *Understanding creativity: The interplay of biological, psychological and social factors*. San Francisco: Jossey-Bass.

Dalai Lama XIV & Chan, V. (2004). *The wisdom of forgiveness*. New York: Riverhead Books.

Dass, R. (1971). *Be here now*. San Cristobal, NM: Lama Foundation.

David, R. (2002). *How to be an adult in relationships*. Boston: Shambhala Publications.

Dawda, D., & Hart, S.D. (2000). Assessing emotional intelligence: Reliability and validity of the Bar-On Emotional Quotient Inventory (EQ-i) in university students. *Personality and Individual Differences, 28*(4), 797–812.

de Jong, P.J., & Peters, M.L. (2007). Contamination vs. harm-relevant outcome expectancies and covariation bias in spider phobia. *Behaviour Research and Therapy, 45*(6), 1271–1284.

de Marneffe, D. (2004). *Maternal desire: On love, children and the inner life*. New York: Little, Brown.

de Montaigne, M. (1995). *The complete essays*. New York: Penguin Classics.

de Shazer, S. (1985). *Keys to solution in brief therapy*. New York: W.W. Norton.

Dewey, J. (1998). Quoted in L. Hickman & T.M. Alexander (Eds.), *The essential Dewey*. Indianapolis: Indiana University Press.

Dillard, J., & Pfau, M. (2002). *The persuasion handbook: Developments in theory and practice*. Newbury Park, CA: Sage Publications.

Dlugos, R., & Friedlander, M. (2001). Passionately committed psychotherapists: A qualitative study of their experience. *Professional Psychology: Research and Practice, 32*(3), 298–304.

Dormaar, M., Dijkman, C., & de Vries, M. (1989). Consensus in patient therapist interactions: A measure of the therapist relationship related to outcome. *Psychotherapy and Psychosomatics, 51*(2), 69–76.

Dowd, E.T., & Leahy, R. (2003). *Clinical advances in cognitive psychotherapy: Theory and application*. New York: Springer Publishing.

Duckro, P.N. (1991). Biofeedback in the management of headache: II. *Headache Quarterly, 2*(1), 7–22.

Edison, T. (1914). *The life of Thomas Edison*. Retrieved June 30, 2007, from http://memory.loc.gov/ammem/edhtml/edbio.html.

Egan, G. (1994). *The skilled helper: A problem-management approach to helping.* Pacific Grove, CA: Brooks/Cole Publishing.

Einstein, A. (2005). In A. Lassieuer, *Albert Einstein: Genius of the twentieth century.* New York: Franklin Watts.

Eliot, G. (1996). *Daniel Deronda.* New York: Penguin Books. (Original work published 1876).

Emerson, R.W. (2006). *Nature addresses and lectures.* Whitefish, MT: Kessinger Publishing. (Original work published 1849).

Enright, R. (2001). *Forgiveness is a choice.* Washington, DC: American Psychological Association.

Erikson, M., Rosen, S., & Hoffman, L. (1982). *My voice will go with you.* New York: W.W. Norton.

Farber, B., Brink, D., & Patricia, R. (Eds.). (1996). *The psychotherapy of Carl Rogers: Cases and commentary.* New York: Guilford Press.

Feltham, C., & Horton, I. (2000). *Handbook of counseling and psychotherapy.* Newbury Park, CA: Sage Publications.

Flanigan, B. (1992). *Forgiving the unforgivable.* New York: MacMillan.

Ford, H. (date unknown). *Quote.* Retrieved June 30, 2007, from http://mlmsuccesscoach.wordpress.com/2007/02/05/think-you-can.

Frank, J. (1973). *Persuasion and healing: A comparative study of psychotherapy.* Baltimore: Johns Hopkins University Press.

Freedman, S., & Enright, R. (1996). Forgiveness as an intervention goal with incest survivors. *Journal of Consulting and Clinical Psychology, 64*(5), 983–992.

Freud, S. (1995, 1989). *The Freud reader* (P. Gay, Ed.). New York: W. W. Norton.

Friedman, M. (2006). *Post-traumatic and acute stress disorders: The latest assessment and treatment strategies.* Kansas City, MO: Compact Clinicals.

Fromm, E. (2000). *Changes in the therapist.* Florence, KY: Lawrence Erlbaum Associates.

Fulghum, R. (1989). *All I really need to know I learned in kindergarten.* New York: Ballantine Books.

Garagnon, F. (1999). *Jade and the sacred mystery of life.* (T. K. Roth, Trans.). Quebec, Canada: Coffragants.

Gartner, J. (2000). Quoted in M. S. Durham, *The therapist's encounters with revenge and forgiveness.* Philadelphia: Jessica Kingsley Publishers.

Gaudiano, B.A., & Miller, I.W. (2006). Patients' expectancies, the alliance in pharmacotherapy, and treatment outcomes in bipolar disorder. *Journal of Consulting and Clinical Psychology, 74*(4), 671–676.

Germer, C., Siegel, R., & Fulton, P. (2005). *Mindfulness and psychotherapy.* New York: Guilford Press.

Gilbert, P. (2000). *Genes on the couch: Explorations in evolutionary psychotherapy.* Philadelphia: Taylor & Francis.

Goldfarb, W., Goldfarb, N., & Scholle, H. (1996). The speech of mothers of schizophrenic children. *American Journal of Psychiatry, 122*(11), 1220–1227.

Goldfried, M., Orlinsky, D., & Ronnestad, M.H. (2000). *How therapists change: Personal and professional reflections.* Washington, DC: American Psychological Association.

Goldsmith, M. (2007). *What got you here won't get you there.* New York: Hyperion.

Goldstein, A. (1996). *The investigation of psychotherapy.* New York: Springer Publishing.

Goleman, D. (1995). *Emotional intelligence.* New York: Bantam Books.

Gratch, A. (2006). *If men could talk: Unlocking the secret language of men.* New York: Little, Brown.

Gray, J. (2002). *Men, women, and relationships: Making peace with the opposite sex.* New York: Harper Paperbacks.

Graybar, S., & Leonard, L. (2005). In defense of listening. *American Journal of Psychotherapy, 59,* 1–18.

Green, J. (2001). *The road to success is paved with failure.* New York: Little, Brown.

Green, S., & Flemons, D. (2004). *Quickies: The handbook of brief sex therapy.* New York: W.W. Norton.

Greenberg, L., & Horvath, A. (1989). Development and validation of the working alliance inventory. *Journal of Counseling Psychology, 36*(2), 223–233.

Greenberg, L., & Johnson, S. (1988). *Emotionally focused therapy for couples.* New York: Guilford Press.

Greenberg, L.S., Watson, J.C., & Elliot, R. (2001). Empathy. *Psychotherapy: Theory, Research, Practice, Training, 38*(4), 380–384.

Greenspan, M. (1993). *A new approach to women and therapy.* New York: TAB Books.

Gurman, A., & Jacobson, N. (2002). *Clinical handbook of couple therapy.* New York: Guilford Press.

Haley, J. (1991). *Problem-solving therapy.* San Francisco: Jossey-Bass.

Hampden-Turner, C. (1971). *Radical man: The process of psycho-social development.* New York: Doubleday.

Hannah, M.T. (2005). *Imago relationship therapy: Perspectives on theory.* San Francisco: Jossey-Bass.

Heraclitus (2003). Fragment #23. *Fragments.* East Rutherford, New Jersey: Penguin. (Circa 500 B.C.E.)

Hermansson, G. (1997). Boundaries and boundary management in counseling: The never-ending story. *British Journal of Guidance and Counselling, 25*(2), 133–146.

Holm, O. (2006). Communication processes in critical systems: Dialogues concerning communications. *Marketing Intelligence and Planning, 24*(5), 493–504.

Hope. B., & Hope, L. (2004). *Bob Hope: My life in jokes.* New York: Hyperion.

Horst, E. (1998). *Recovering the lost self: Healing for victims of clergy sexual abuse.* Collegeville, MN: Liturgical Press.

Houston, J. (1998). *A passion for the possible: A guide to realizing your true potential.* New York: HarperCollins.

Hoyt, M. (2000). *Some stories are better than others: Doing what works best in brief therapy and managed care.* Philadelphia: Brunner/Mazel.

Hoyt, M., Rosenbaum, R., & Talman, M. (1992). Planned single session therapy. In S. Budman, M. Hoyt, & S. Friedman (Eds.), *The first session in brief therapy.* New York: Guilford Press.

Hughes, M., Patterson, L., Bonita, T., & Bradford, J. (2005). *Emotional intelligence in action: Training and coaching activities for leaders and managers.* San Francisco: Pfeiffer.

Huxley, T.H. (2007). *Lay sermons, addresses and reviews.* Charleston, SC: BiblioBazaar. (Original work published 1870).

Jennings, L., Sovereign, A., & Bottorff, N. (2005). Nine ethical values of master therapists. *Journal of Mental Health Counseling, 27*(1), 32–47.

Johnson, D. (1991). Attitude Modification Methods. In F. Kanfer & A. Goldstein (Eds.), *Helping people change,* (pp. 58–91). New York: Allyn and Bacon.

Jones, M. (1998). *The thinker's toolkit.* New York: Three Rivers Press.

Jung, C. (1999). In M. Anthony, *Jung's circle of women.* New York: Weiser Books.

Kabat-Zinn, J. (1994). *Wherever you go there you are: Mindfulness meditation in everyday life.* New York: Hyperion.

Kadushin, G. (1996). Gay men with AIDS and their families of origin: An analysis of social support. *Health & Social Work, 21*(2), 141–149.

Kahn, S., & Fromm, E. (2000). *Changes in the therapist.* Florence, KY: Lawrence Erlbaum Associates.

Kandel, E. (2005). *Psychiatry, psychoanalysis, and the new science of mind.* Arlington, VA: American Psychiatric Publishing.

Kanfer, F., & Goldstein, A. (1980). *Helping people change.* New York: Pergamon.

Kang, L., & Albion, M. (2005). *Passion at work: How to find the work you love and live the time of your life.* Upper Saddle River, NJ: Prentice Hall.

Karasu, T.B. (1992). *Wisdom in the practice of psychotherapy.* New York: Basic Books.

Karter, J. (2002). *On training to become a therapist.* Berkshire, United Kingdom: Open University Press.

Kassen, L. (1996). *Second opinions: Sixty patients evaluate their therapists.* New York: Jacob Aronson.

Kazantzis, N., & L'Abate, L. (2007). *Handbook of homework assignments in psychotherapy: Research, practice, and prevention.* New York: Springer Publishing.

Keen, S. (1992). *Fire in the belly: On being a man.* New York: Bantam Books.

Keeney, B. (2005). *Improvisational therapy.* Guilford Press.

Kelly, G. (1963). *Theories of personality: The psychology of personal constructs.* New York: W.W. Norton.

Kerry, J. (2006, Oct 30). Speech given at Democratic campaign rally, Pasadena, CA.

Khanna, P., & Vohra, S.S. (2000). Psychological exploration of the relationship between emotional intelligence and job success in an IT company. *Journal of the Indian Academy of Applied Psychology, 29*(1–2), 73–82.

King, M. (1964). *A testimony of hope: The essential speeches and writings of Martin Luther King, Jr.* San Francisco: HarperSanFrancisco.

Kottler, J., & Carlson, J. (2002). *Bad therapy: Master therapists share their worst failures.* Philadelphia: Brunner-Routledge.

Kottler, J. (2003). *On being a therapist.* San Francisco: Jossey-Bass.

Krasner, B., & Joyce, A. (1995). *Truth, trust, and relationships: Healing interventions in contextual therapy.* New York: Brunner/Mazel.

Krupp, G., Genovese, F. & Krupp, T. (1986). To have and have not: Multiple identifications in pathological bereavement. *Journal of the American Academy of Psychoanalysis and Dynamic Psychiatry, 14*(3), 337–348.

Kwee, M. (1990). *Psychotherapy, meditation and health.* Isleworth, Middlesex, U.K.: East-West Publications.

Lambert, K. (2005). *Clinical neuroscience and improving mind and brain.* New York: Worth Publishers.

Lao Tzu. (Circa 600 B.C.E.). *Tao Te Ching.*

Lazarus, A. (1989). *The practice of multimodal therapy.* Baltimore: Johns Hopkins University Press.

Lazarus, A. (1997). *Brief but comprehensive psychotherapy.* New York: Springer Publishing.

Leahy, R., & Dowd, E.T. (2003). *Clinical advances in cognitive psychotherapy: Theory and application.* New York: Springer Publishing.

Lerner, H. (1989). *Women in therapy.* New York: Harper Paperbacks.

Levine, E. (2004). *Tending the fire: Studies in art, therapy, and creativity.* Ontario, Canada: EGS Press.

Lipchik, E. (2002). *Beyond technique in solution-focused therapy: Working with emotions and the therapeutic relationship.* New York: Guilford Press.

London, P. (1964). *The modes and morals of psychotherapy.* Austin, TX: Holt, Rinehart and Winston.

Lynn, A. (2004). *The EQ difference: Putting emotional intelligence to work.* New York: American Management Associations.

MacDougal, A.F. (1928). *The autobiography of a business woman.* New York: Little, Brown.

Madanes, C. (1992). Stories of psychotherapy. In J. Zeig (Ed.), *The evolution of psychotherapy: The second conference* (pp. 39–50). New York: Brunner/Mazel.

Madden, J. (1984). *Hey, wait a minute, I wrote a book!* New York: Villard.

Mahoney, M. (2003). *Constructive psychotherapy: A practical guide.* New York: Guilford Press.

Manz, C. (2002). *The power of failure: 27 ways to turn life's setbacks into success.* San Francisco: Berrett-Koehler.

Maslach, C. (2003). *Burnout: The cost of caring.* Cambridge: Malor Books.

Maslow, A. (1991). Quoted in R.J. Decarvalho, *The founders of humanistic psychology.* Westport, CT: Praeger.

May, R. (1989). *Love and will.* New York: W.W. Norton.

McCullough, L. (2005). *Changing character: Short-term anxiety regulating psychotherapy.* New York: Basic Books.

McGoldrick, M., Giordano, J., & Garcia-Preto, N. (1996). *Ethnicity and family therapy.* New York: Guilford Press.

McMillan, D. (2005). *Emotion rituals: A resource for therapists and clients.* New York: Routledge.

Meichenbaum, D. (2005). Thirty-five years of working with suicidal patients: Lessons learned. *Canadian Psychology, 46*(2), 64–72.

Mejia, X.E. (2005). Gender matters: Working with adult male survivors of trauma. *Journal of Counseling and Development, 83*(1), 29–40.

Menninger, K.A. (1985). *Man against himself.* Orlando: Harcourt.

Meth, R., Pasick, R., Gordon, B., & Allen, J. (2006). *Men in therapy: The challenge.* New York: Guilford Press.

Meyeroff, M. (1971). *On caring.* New York: Harper and Row.

Meyerwitz, J. (1998). In R.B. Cialdini, *Influence: The psychology of persuasion.* New York: William Morrow.

Milgram, S. (1963). Behavioral study of obedience. *Journal of Abnormal and Social Psychology, 67*(4), 371–378.

Miller, R. (2005). Suffering in psychology: The demoralization of psychotherapeutic practice. *Journal of Psychotherapy Integration, 15*(3), 299–336.

Monk, G., Winslade, J., Crocket, K., & Epstom, D. (1996). *Narrative therapy in practice: The archaeology of hope.* San Francisco: Jossey-Bass.

Montagu, A. (1988). Quotation 2856. *Contemporary quotations* (J.P. Simpson, Ed.). Boston: Houghton Mifflin.

Morstyn, R. (2002). The therapist's dilemma: Be sincere or fake it? *Australasian Psychiatry, 10*(4), 325–329.

Myers, W. (1982). *Shrink dreams: The secret longings, fantasies, and prejudices of therapists and how they affect their patients.* New York: Simon and Schuster.

Newman, C.F., Leahy, R.L., Beck, A.T., Reilly-Harrington, N., & Gyulai G. (2001). *Bipolar disorder: A cognitive therapy approach.* Washington, DC: American Psychological Association.

Nitza, A. (2005). Mechanisms of change: The contributions of Rex Stockton. *Journal for Specialists in Group Work, 30*(3), 271–281.

Noonan, M. (1998). Understanding the "difficult" patient from a dual person perspective. *Clinical Social Work Journal, 26*(2), 129–141.

Norcross, J. (2002). *Psychotherapy relationships that work: Therapist contributions and responsiveness to patients.* New York: Oxford University Press.

Norcross, J., Prochaska, J., & DiClemente, C. (1994). *Changing for good: A revolutionary six stage program for overcoming bad habits and moving your life positively forward.* New York: Avon Books.

O'Hanlon, W.H., & O'Hanlon, B. (2003). *A guide to inclusive therapy.* New York: W.W. Norton.

Orlinsky, D., Botermans, J., & Ronnestad, M. (2001). Towards an empirically grounded model of psychotherapy training: Four thousand psychotherapists rate influences on their development. *Australian Psychologist, 36*(2), 139–148.

Parkes, C. (2001). *Bereavement: Studies of grief in adult life.* New York: Routledge.

Patton, J. (1985). *Is human forgiveness possible?* Nashville: Abingdon Press.

Perry, D., Perry, L., & Rasmussen, P. (1986). Cognitive social learning mediators of aggression. *Child Development, 57*(3), 700–711.

Peterson, C. (2006). *A primer in positive psychology.* New York: Oxford University Press.

Pipher, M. (2003). *Letters to a young therapist.* New York: Basic Books.

Poincare, J.H. (2003). *Science and method.* Austin, TX: Dover Publications. (Original work published 1914).

Pope, K., & Vasquez, M. (1998). *Ethics in psychotherapy and counseling: A practical guide.* San Francisco: Jossey-Bass.

Potter-Efron, P.S., & Potter-Efron, R.T. (1999). *The secret message of shame: Pathways to hope and healing.* Oakland, CA: New Harbinger Publications.

Quick, E. (1996). *Doing what works in brief therapy: A strategic solution focused approach.* Burlington, MA: Academic Press.

Rabinor, J. (2002). *A starving madness: Tales of hunger, hope and healing in psychotherapy.* Carlsbad, CA: Gurze Books.

Rabinowitz, I., (Ed.). (1998). *Inside therapy: Illuminating writings about therapists, patients, and psychotherapy.* New York: St. Martin's/Griffin.

Real, T. (1998). *I don't want to talk about it: Overcoming the secret legacy of male depression.* New York: Fireside.

Richo, D. (2002). *How to be an adult in relationships: The five keys to mindful loving.* Boston: Shambala Publications, Inc.

Rilke, R.M. (2002). *Letters to a young poet.* Mineola, NY: Dover Publications. (Original work published 1903).

Roach, M.S. (1997). *Caring from the heart: The convergence of caring and spirituality.* Mahwah, NJ: Paulist Press.

Rochefoucauld, F. Duc de La. (2004). #148. *Moral maxims and reflections.* Whitefish, MT: Kessinger Publications. (Original work published 1665–1678).

Rogers, C. (1961). *On becoming a person: A therapist's view of psychotherapy.* New York: Houghton Mifflin.

Rubie-Davies, C.M. (2007). Classroom interactions: Exploring the practices of high- and low-expectation teachers. *British Journal of Educational Psychology, 77*(2), 289–306.

Russel, S., & Carey, M. (2004). *Narrative therapy: Responding to your questions.* Minneapolis: Narrative Books.

Sabine, W., & Steketee, G.S. (2006). *Cognitive therapy for obsessive-compulsive disorder: A guide for professionals.* Oakland, CA: New Harbinger Publications, Inc.

Salovey, P. (2003). *Social psychology of health.* New York: Psychology Press.

Schilling, J., & Crisafulli, C. (2006). *Me and a guy named Elvis: My lifelong friendship with Elvis Presley.* New York: Gotham.

Schon, D. (2003). *The reflective practitioner: How professionals think in action.* New York: Basic Books.

Schreiner, O. (2006). *Dreams.* Lenox, MA: Hard Press Editions.

Schwartz, J., & Begley, S. (2003). *The mind and the brain: Neuroplasticity and the power of mental force.* New York: Regan Books.

Schwartz-Borden, G. (1986). Grief work: Prevention and intervention. *Social Casework, 67*(8), 499–505.

Segal, J. (1997). *Raising your emotional intelligence: A practical guide.* New York: Owl Books.

Seligman, M. (2006). *Mentoring brilliant students.* Presentation at the 114th Annual Convention of the American Psychological Association, New Orleans, LA.

Shakespeare, W. (1997). *Macbeth.* New York: Cambridge University Press. (Original work published 1603-1606).

Shaw, G.B. (2005). *Man and Superman.* Fairfield, Iowa: 1st World Publishing. (Original work published 1903).

Sherman, R. (1991). *Solving problems in couples and family therapy.* New York: Brunner/Mazel.

Shore, L. (1995). *Tending inner gardens: The healing art of feminist psychotherapy.* Binghamton, NY: Haworth Press.

Silverstein, O., & Rashbaum, B. (1995). *The courage to raise good men.* New York: Viking Press.

Skovholt, T. (1995). *The evolving professional: Self stages and themes in therapist and counselor development.* New York: John Wiley & Sons.

Skovholt, T. (2001). *The resilient practitioner: Burnout prevention and self-care strategies for counselors, therapists, teachers, and health professionals.* Boston: Allyn & Bacon.

Skovholt, T. (2005). The cycle of caring: A model of expertise in the helping professions. *Journal of Mental Health Counseling, 27*(1), 82–93.

Skovholt, T., & Jennings, L. (2005). Mastery and expertise in counseling. *Journal of Mental Health Counseling, 27*(1), 13–18.

Smedes, L. (1996). *Forgive and forget: Healing the hurts we don't deserve.* New York: HarperCollins.

Solomon, M., & Siegel, D. (2003). *Healing trauma: Attachment, mind, body and brain.* New York: W.W. Norton.

Sommers-Flannagan, J., & Sommers-Flannagan, R. (2002). *Clinical interviewing.* New York: John Wiley & Sons.

Stein, G. (date unknown). *Gertrude Stein Famous Quotes.* Retrieved July 2, 2007, from http://www.quotemountain.com/famous_quote_author/gertrude_stein_famous_quotations/.

Stern, E.M. (1991). *Psychotherapy and the poverty patient.* Binghamton, NY: Haworth Press.

Strean, H. (1993). *The use of humor in psychotherapy.* New York: Jason Aronson.

Strupp, H., & Bloxom, A. (1973). Preparing lower class patients for psychotherapy: Development and evaluation of a role-induction film. *Journal of Consulting and Clinical Psychology, 41*(3), 373–384.

Sue, D.W., & Sue, D. (2003). *Counseling the culturally diverse: Theory and practice.* New York: John Wiley & Sons.

Taibbi, R. (1996). *Doing family therapy: Craft and creativity in clinical practice.* New York: Guilford Press.

Talmon, M. (1990). *Single session therapy: Maximizing the effect of the first (and often only) therapeutic encounter.* Somerset, NJ: John Wiley & Sons, Inc.

Tangey, J.P. (2000). In S. Berg (Ed.), *Natural prescriptions for women: What to do — and when to do it — to solve more than 100 female health problems — without drugs* (pp. 308–309). Emmaus, PA: Rodale Press, Inc.

Tarrier, N., Wells, A., & Haddock, G. (2000). *Treating complex cases: The cognitive behavioral therapy approach.* New York: John Wiley & Sons.

Teresa, M. (1992, December). Quoted in R.F. Kennedy, Jr., *Rolling Stone.*

Teresa, M. (1997). *Mother Teresa: In my own words.* New York: Gramercy.

Thorne, B. (2002). *The mystical path of person-centered therapy: Hope beyond despair.* Philadelphia: Whurr Publishers.

Tutu, D. (2000). *No future without forgiveness.* New York: Image.

Twain, M. (2003). *Mark Twain's autobiography.* Whitefish, MT: Kessinger Publishing. (Original work published 1871).

Villenueve, C. (2001). *Emphasizing the interpersonal in psychotherapy: Families and groups in the era of cost containment.* Philadelphia: Brunner-Routledge.

Wachtel, P. (1993). *Therapeutic communication: Knowing what to say when.* New York: Guilford Press.

Wade, N., Bailey, D., & Schaffer, P. (2005). Helping clients heal: Does forgiveness make a difference? *Professional Psychology: Research and Practice, 36*(6), 636–641.

Walen, S., Digiuseppe, R., & Dryden, W. (1992). *A practitioner's guide to rational emotive therapy.* New York: Oxford University Press.

Wallis, J. (2005). *Faith works: How to live your beliefs and ignite positive social change.* New York: Random House.

Wampold, B. (2001). *The great psychotherapy debate: Models, methods, and findings.* Florence, KY: Lawrence Erlbuam Associates.

Watkins, C.E., & Schneider, L. (1991). *Research in counseling.* Florence, KY: Lawrence Erlbaum Associates.

Webster, M. (1991). Emotional abuse in therapy. *Australian and New Zealand Journal of Family Therapy, 12*(3), 137–145.

Weinberg, G. (2000). The taboo scarf. In I. Rabinowitz (Ed.), *Inside therapy: Illuminating writings about therapists, patients, and psychotherapy.* New York: St. Martin's Griffin.

Whipple, J., Lambert, M., & Vermeersch, D. (2003). Improving the effects of psychotherapy: The use of early identification of treatment and problem-solving strategies in routine practice. *Journal of Counseling Psychology, 50*(1), 59–63.

Winfrey, O. (2006, Jan 6). *The Oprah Winfrey Show.*

Wooden, J. (2005, Nov 22). *Los Angeles Times,* p. D12.

Worden, J.W. (2001). *Grief counseling and grief therapy: A handbook for the mental health professional.* New York: Springer Publishing.

Wrightsman, L. (1992). *Assumptions about human nature: Implications for researcher and practitioner.* Newbury Park, CA: Sage Publications.

Yalom, I. (1980). *Existential therapy.* New York: Basic Books.

Yalom, I. (2003). *The gift of therapy: An open letter to a new generation of therapists and their patients.* New York: HarperPerennial.

Index

The Practical Therapist Series®

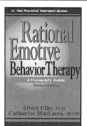

Rational Emotive Behavior Therapy
A Therapist's Guide (Second Edition)
Albert Ellis, Ph.D. and Catharine MacLaren, M.S.W., CEAP
Hardcover: $24.95   176 pages   ISBN: 978-1-886230-61-3
Up-to-date guidebook by the innovator of Rational Emotive Behavior Therapy. Includes thorough description of REBT theory and procedures, case examples, exercises.

Divorce Doesn't Have to Be That Way
A Handbook for The Helping Professional
Jane Appell, Ph.D.
Softcover: $27.95   288 pages   ISBN: 978-1-886230-71-2
A comprehensive therapist's guide to divorce counseling. Emphasizes healthy, family-centered, non-adversarial approach. Key topics: understanding the divorce process, treating "problem" personalities, domestic abuse, custody, legal issues, and more.

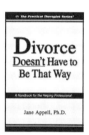

The Soul of Counseling
A New Model for Understanding Human Experience
Dwight Webb, Ph.D.
Softcover: $24.95   192 pages   ISBN: 978-1-886230-59-0
Practical, down-to-earth aids to integrate into professional psychotherapy practice to help deal with clients' issues of the human spirit.

Defusing the High-Conflict Divorce
A Treatment Guide for Working with Angry Couples
Bernard Gaulier, Ph.D., Judith Margerum, Ph.D.
Jerome A. Price, M.A., and James Windell, M.A.
Softcover: $27.95   272 pages   ISBN: 978-1-886230-67-5
The therapist's practical guide for working with angry divorcing couples, offering a unique set of proven programs for quelling the hostility in high-conflict co-parenting couples, and "defusing" their emotional struggles.

Since 1970 — Psychology you can use, from professionals you can trust.

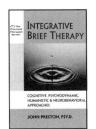

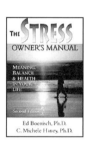